COLORED PENCIL

A PLAYFUL GUIDE TO DRAWING WITH COLORED PENCIL ON THE GO!

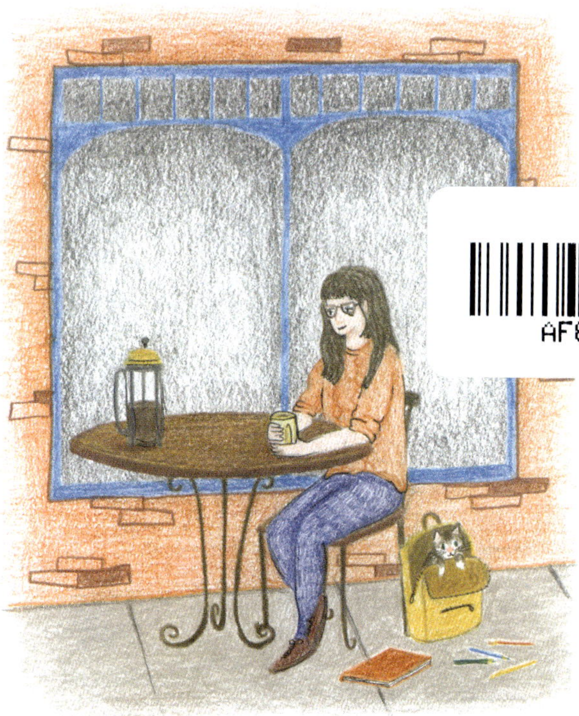

Cara Hanley

Walter Foster

Inspiring | Educating | Creating | Entertaining

Brimming with creative inspiration, how-to projects, and useful information to enrich your everyday life, Quarto Knows is a favorite destination for those pursuing their interests and passions. Visit our site and dig deeper with our books into your area of interest: Quarto Creates, Quarto Cooks, Quarto Homes, Quarto Lives, Quarto Drives, Quarto Explores, Quarto Gifts, or Quarto Kids.

First Published in 2018 by Walter Foster Publishing, an imprint of The Quarto Group.
6 Orchard Road, Suite 100, Lake Forest, CA 92630, USA.
T (949) 380-7510 **F** (949) 380-7575 **www.QuartoKnows.com**

Walter Foster Publishing titles are also available at discount for retail, wholesale, promotional, and bulk purchase. For details, contact the Special Sales Manager by email at specialsales@quarto.com or by mail at The Quarto Group, Attn: Special Sales Manager, 401 Second Avenue North, Suite 310, Minneapolis, MN 55401 USA.

ISBN: 978-1-63322-494-0

Digital edition published in 2018
eISBN: 978-1-63322-495-7

Project Editor: Kyra Wojdyla
Page Layout: Krista Joy Johnson

Printed in China
10 9 8 7 6 5 4 3 2 1

FSC www.fsc.org MIX Paper from responsible sources FSC® C104723

TABLE OF CONTENTS

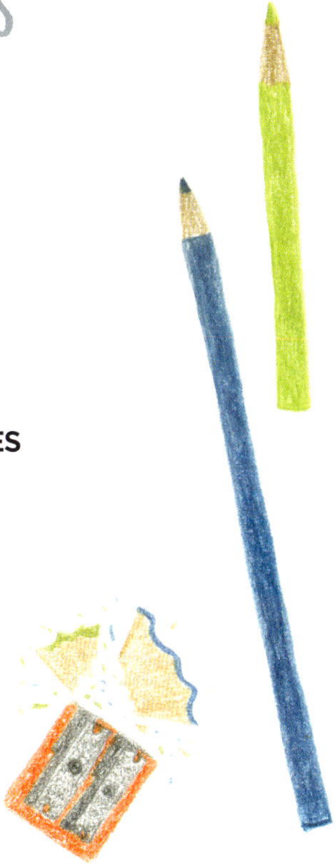

INTRODUCTION

Hello! My name is Cara. I am an illustrator living in upstate New York, and I'm excited to share my passion for colored pencils with you! Art is an integral part of who I am, and it is something that I look forward to creating every day. I delight in every part of the art-making process. It provides me with a deeper connection to the world around me and an escape from the stressors of everyday life.

My routine during the week is to drop my bags when I get home from work and sit down at my drawing table or pack up my tools and materials and head to the park or my favorite café. Weekends are special because they let me take advantage of the late and midmorning sun, which I believe is the best lighting in which to draw and paint. There is nothing like heading out into that magical light with my art supplies and coffee in tow (after some groggy snuggles with my cat, Zipper, of course!).

Inspiration is a necessary ingredient in the recipe for creating art. For me, inspiration comes more easily when I'm immersed in the energy of the community, whether it's my favorite coffee house, a public garden, or a gallery.

As an artist, you will find your own sources of inspiration. This book will guide you through a variety of exercises that focus on subjects both near and far. We will start in your home, head out on some local adventures, and even explore art making while traveling.

To hone your drawing skills, I recommend practicing every day. This will help you develop a natural ease with your colored pencils and it's one of the best ways to establish your own style. If you draw enough, your style will develop organically!

As you work through this book, allow yourself to play without judgment. Draw in different places. Listen to music when you draw, and then draw in silence. Draw in the morning. Draw at night. Draw with your nondominant hand for a bit. Draw with your cat on your desk (but watch your water glass!).

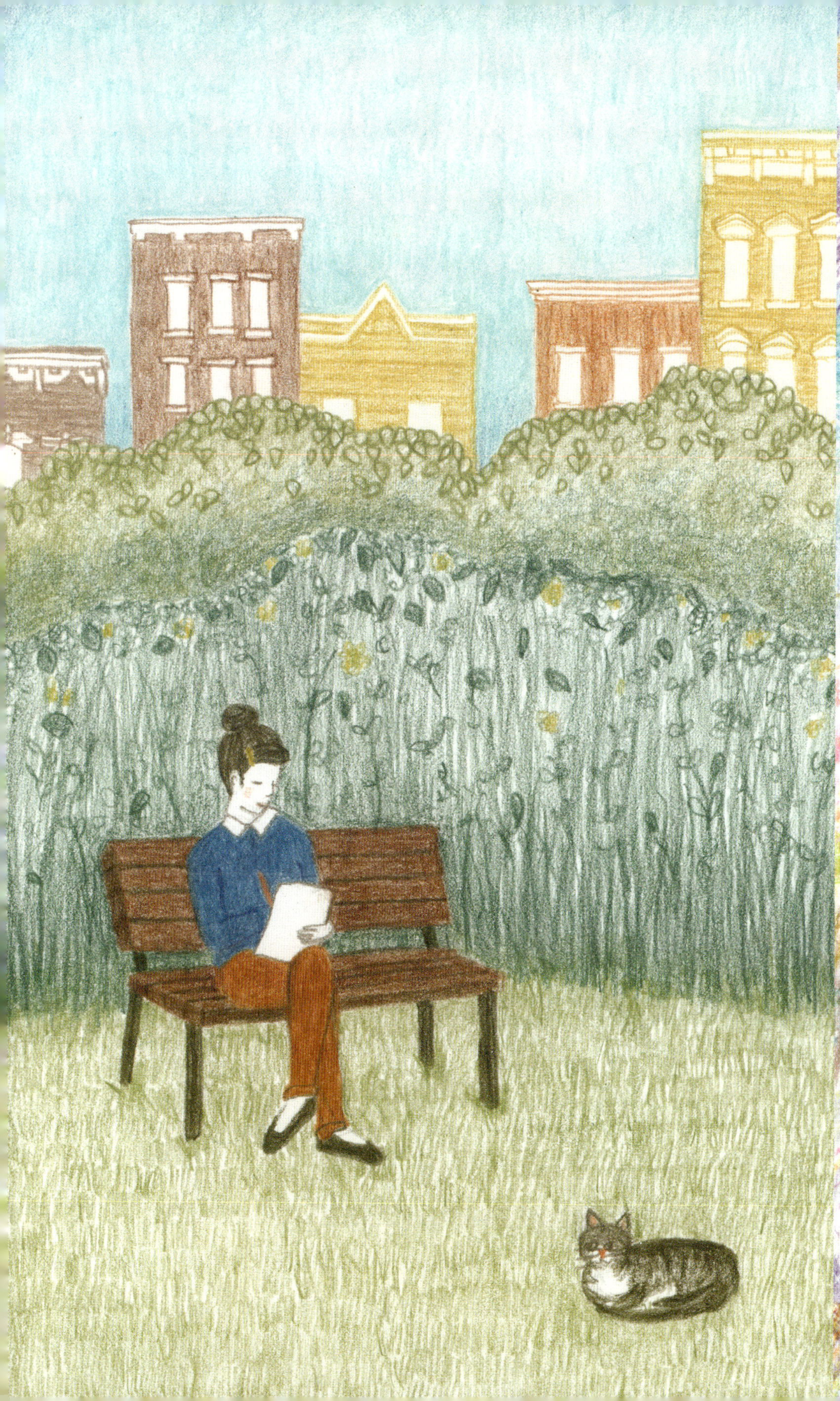

TOOLS & MATERIALS

Let's talk art supplies! First and foremost, let's talk about the star of the show.

COLORED PENCILS

There are two main types of colored pencils: wax and oil. Wax and oil are the agents that bind the pigment together to form a colored pencil. Wax colored pencils are generally more convenient to find and also less expensive. Oil colored pencils are more expensive but easier to sharpen and less prone to breaking. I've worked with both and genuinely enjoy both kinds. If you can, test out both wax and oil colored pencils at your local art store before committing to one or the other.

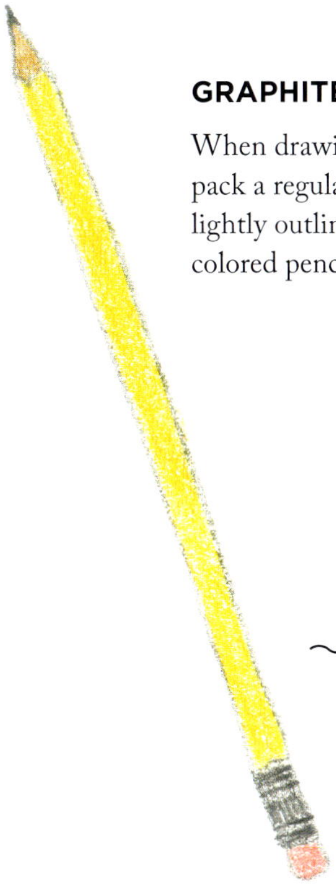

GRAPHITE PENCIL

When drawing with colored pencils, I always pack a regular graphite pencil. I use this pencil to lightly outline my drawing before committing to colored pencil, which I can't erase.

Because of its silvery sheen, you can also use your graphite pencil for drawing metallic details.

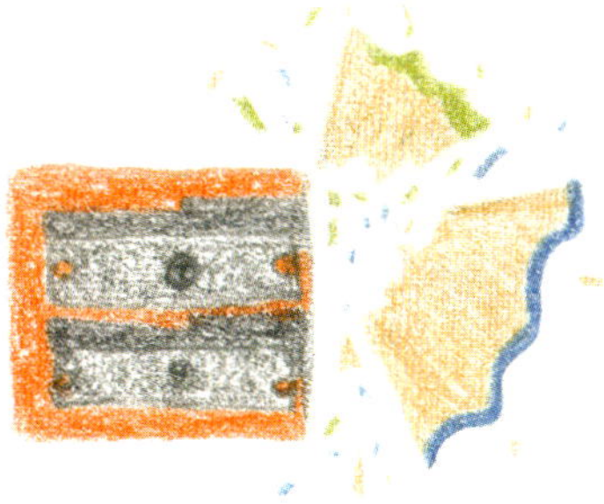

SHARPENER

You may have a pencil sharpener lying around from your school days. Remember sharpening all those #2 pencils in preparation for a test? That sharpener will likely do the trick, but if you don't have one, I recommend getting a pencil sharpener that is covered (unlike the one illustrated). As you work through this book, you will sharpen your colored pencils a lot. Having a covered sharpener will prevent undue mess.

PAPER

When it comes to colored pencil, paper is our canvas! Therefore, it's important to choose a quality paper that takes well to colored pencil. The "tooth" of a paper refers to the roughness. Having some tooth to your paper is important when working with colored pencil. The colored pencil pigment needs something to grab onto to stick to the paper and stay in place.

If you go to your local art store, you may be able to find paper that is designed specifically for drawing with colored pencils, but an alternative is hot-pressed watercolor paper. You will find that a notebook is more convenient for carrying on the go.

You can tell if a paper has tooth or not by lightly touching the surface of it.

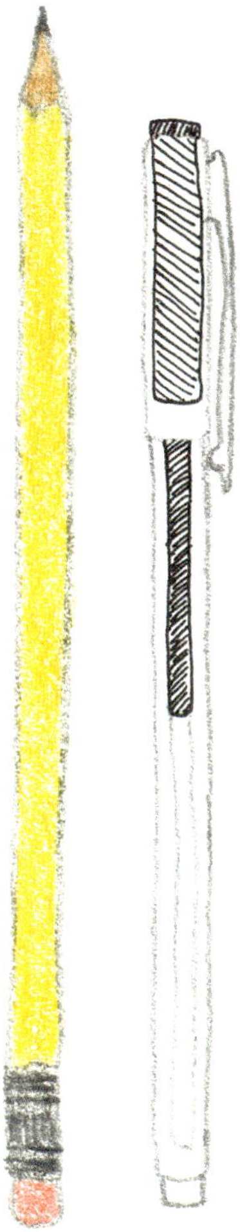

PEN

I always have a felt-tip black pen in my pencil case. These pens are great for adding details to drawings and creating a sharper edge or deeper shadow. A pen is also useful to have on hand if you are keeping a drawing journal and want to write little notes or thoughts next to your images.

PENCIL CASE

You have a lot of flexibility with the pencil case you choose. I suggest finding one that inspires you! My pencil case is canvas, has many pockets, and is mustard yellow and blue (one of my favorite color combinations).

Take some time finding a pencil case that feels good to you. I recommend getting a fabric pencil case because it will prevent breakage of your colored pencils. Make sure the pencil case is long enough to fit your colored pencils with some wiggle room to spare!

DRAWING TECHNIQUES

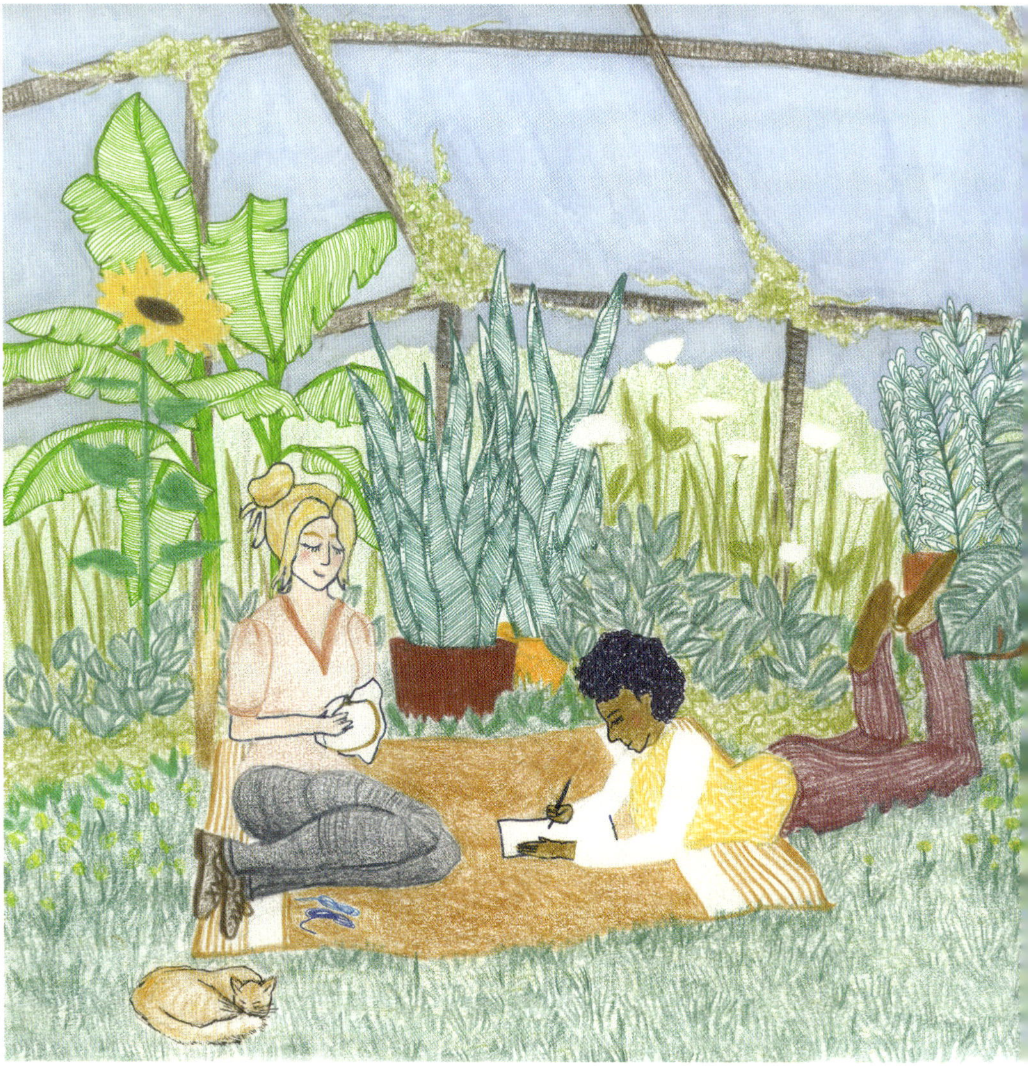

Before jumping into the step-by-step exercises in this book, it is important to learn the basic techniques of contour, fill, and texturing. While contours create structure in a drawing, fill and texture add depth and richness. Once mastered, these skills will allow you to create richness and depth in your work and to achieve a more sophisticated level of drawing.

One advantage of selecting colored pencil as a medium is that the drawing techniques are relatively easy to learn, yet they permit a wide range of artistic effects. Before you know it, you'll be using texturing and fill techniques—such as shading, hatching, stippling, stroking, and layering—to make your art come alive!

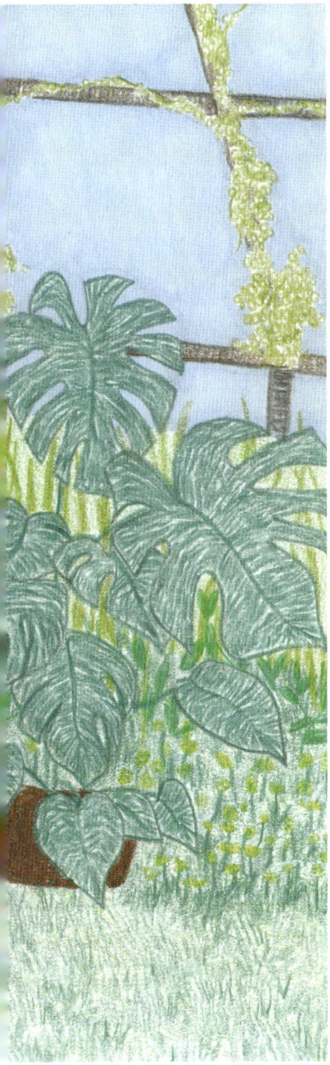

CONTOUR

Contouring essentially means outlining. Contouring is the first step to laying the framework of your drawing.

You can practice drawing contours using a technique called "blind contouring." Pick out a simple object, like a coffee cup or piece of fruit, and draw the outline of the item without looking down at your paper or picking up your pencil. Pretend that your gaze is an ant crawling over the outline of the object, and sync the movement of your pencil with your gaze. Don't worry if this feels awkward and your drawing isn't very good—the exercise will help develop your hand-eye coordination with the pencil and will improve your ability to observe detail in objects.

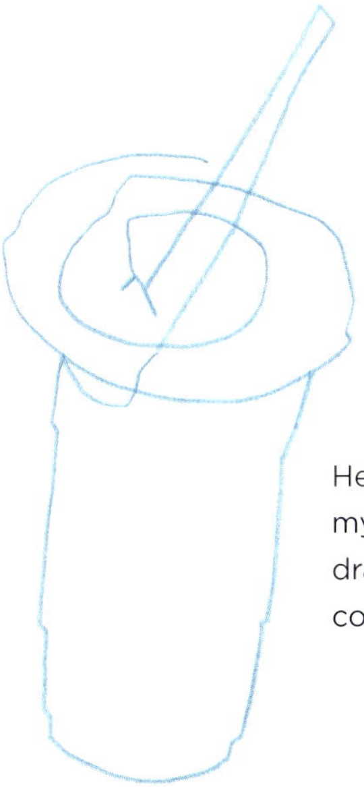

Here you can see my blind contour drawing of my iced coffee cup!

When blind contouring, remember that your brain has an idea of what an object should look like and can override the reality of the object.

TEXTURE

Texture is my favorite element to add to a drawing because adding the right texture can really make a drawing pop! When drawing with colored pencil, texture is created by using different line strokes.

Choose a colored pencil, and practice drawing lines in any shape with varying pressures. Pay close attention to how the lines thicken and sometimes soften when your pencil is less sharp versus the crisp and dark thin lines created by a freshly sharpened pencil.

Softened Point

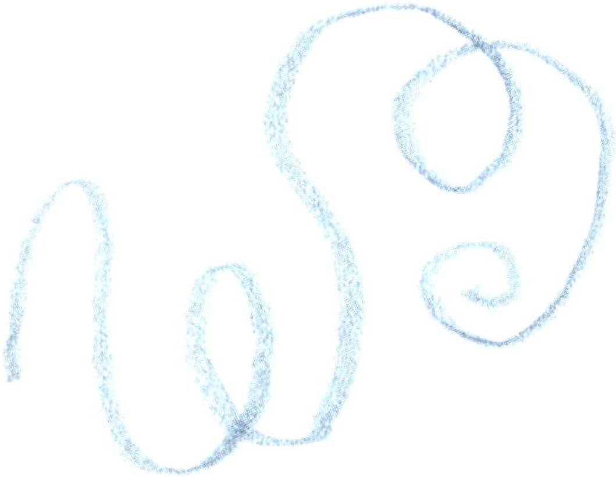

Sharp Point

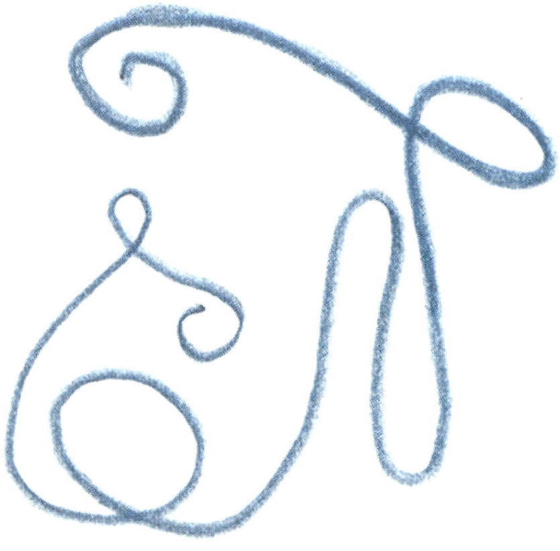

For a unique touch, use any of the texture techniques to fill a shape with color.

HATCHING & CROSSHATCHING

Hatching and crosshatching are two easy ways to add texture to a drawing. Hatching consists of repeated, parallel straight lines. Practice hatching by using different lengths and directions of lines. Crosshatching consists of crossed, parallel straight lines.

Hatching

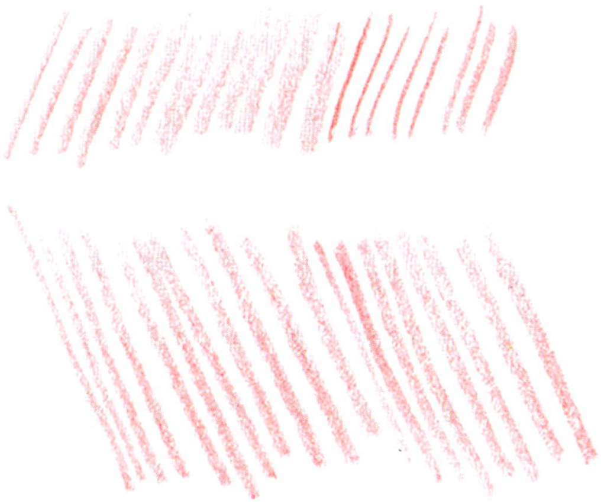

Crosshatching

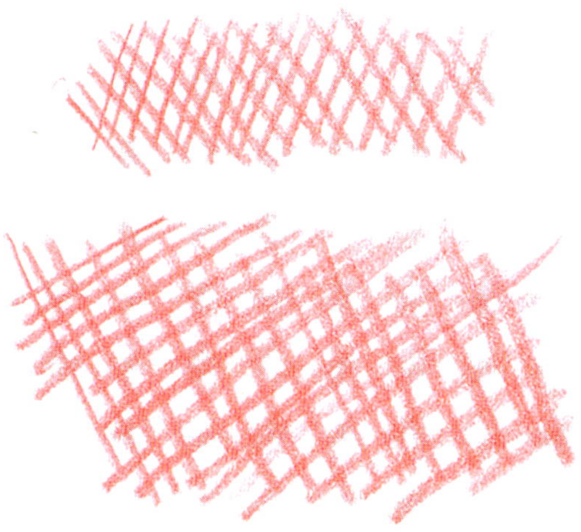

To create a deeper value of a color, crosshatch using a single color. You can also crosshatch using multiple colors that will optically mix together.

STIPPLING

Stippling is another great way to create texture in your drawings. Stippling is performed by repeatedly making little dots within an area of a drawing. The denser the dots, the more saturated that field of color will appear. Try stippling with different densities of dots, and see the effect this creates.

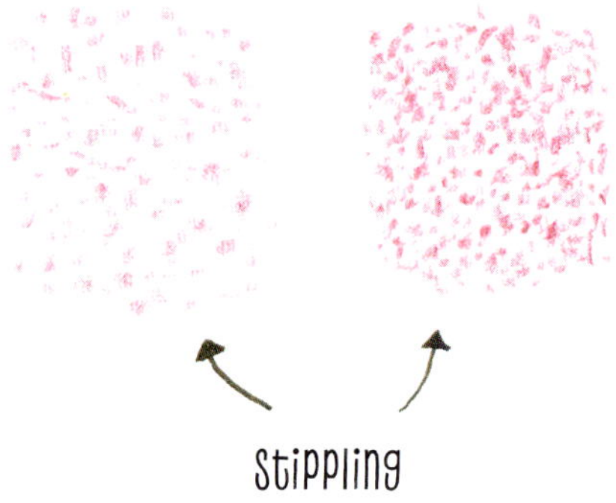

Stippling requires patience, but it can create a successful impact when used correctly!

FILL

After you finish contouring the subjects of your drawings, you may need to fill those spaces with fields of color. Two ways to fill in these contoured shapes are by stroking and scumbling.

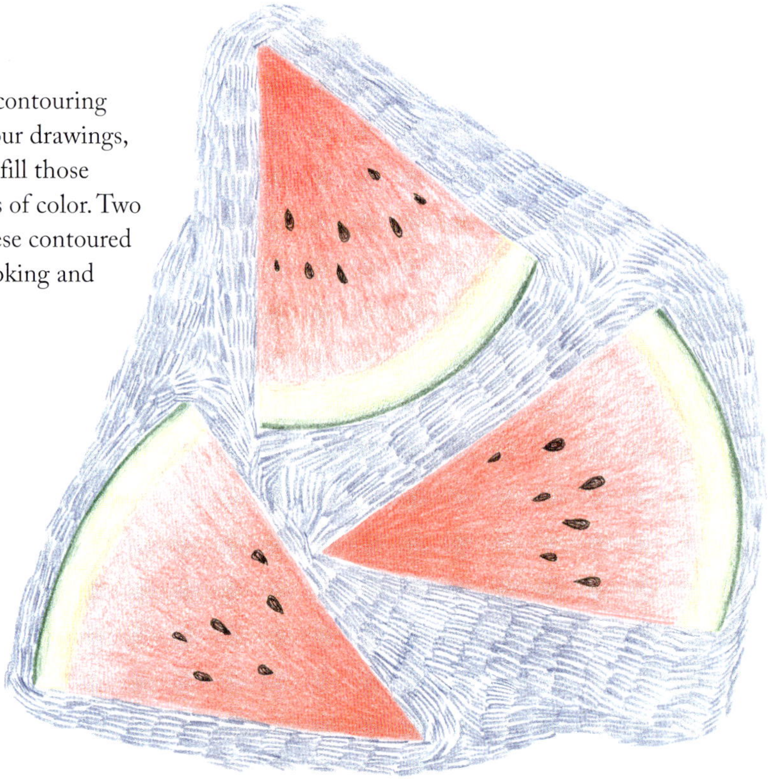

STROKING & SCUMBLING

When using stroking to fill your image, you will move your colored pencil in a back-and-forth motion. Do you remember coloring in coloring books as a child? Chances are you were stroking and scumbling without even knowing it! When using stroking to fill an image, you move your colored pencil in a back-and-forth motion. To scumble, use circular, scribbling movements to fill the image.

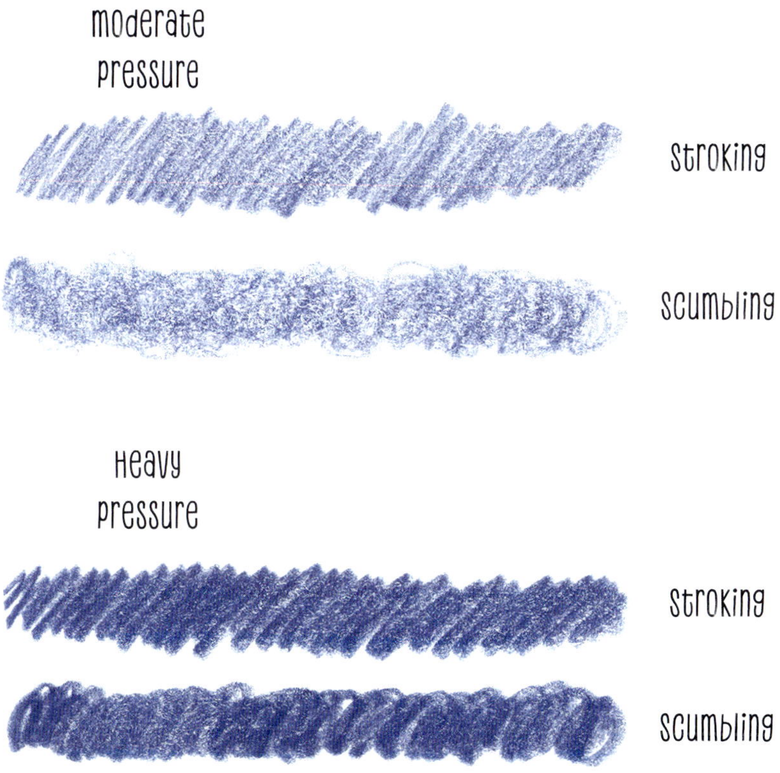

Scumbling can be used to express movement, add excitement, or create texture in subjects like grass and landscapes.

SHADING

Shading creates dimensionality in an image. If you are going for realism, shading is a must. If you are using a more illustrative style in your artwork, you can use shading in moderation or not at all. Shading can be created with colored pencil by using varying pressure or saturation, and by layering.

PRESSURE & SATURATION

One way to create the appearance of a shadow in your image is by playing with the saturation of the color you are using. More saturated areas appear as shadows and tend to recede into the drawing. Lighter areas indicate highlights. Using more pressure will create a more saturated result. You can also do multiple layers using moderate pressure to create a similar effect.

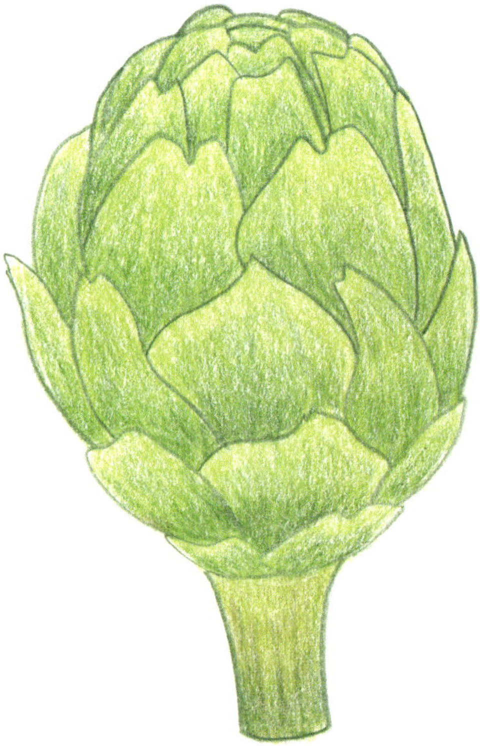

LAYERING

Another way to shade an image is by layering colors. Colored pencils are unique in that you cannot blend them, but instead you layer colors on top of one another to create the hue or shade you desire. It is most effective to layer dark on top of light instead of vice versa because you have more control that way.

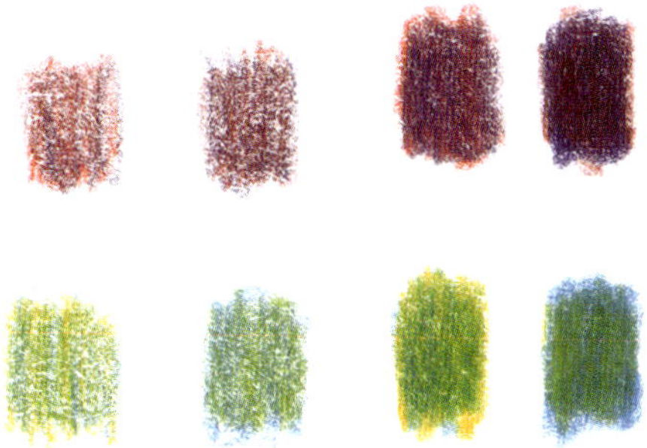

I do not tend to use black or grays to create shadows when drawing with colored pencils because I find it can lead to a muddy result. Try layering a similar but darker color for the shadow. For instance, you may layer a yellow ochre color to create the shadow on a banana. A more striking approach to creating a shadow is by layering a darker color that is not analogous (see page 20) to the base color of the image.

Sometimes when I'm having a creative block, I like to practice these techniques by filling a whole page with different fills and textures. Open to a fresh page in your sketchbook, and choose a few of your favorite colored pencils to practice these techniques!

COLOR THEORY BASICS

Color theory helps us to understand how colors relate to one another. Certain colors work together better than others to convey a particular mood in a drawing. Choosing the right colors can make the difference between a good drawing and a great drawing.

When you narrow down the limitless choices of the color wheel to a particular selection of colors, you have created the color palette for your drawing. Understanding color theory is essential to developing effective color palettes.

In this chapter, we will experiment with developing different color palettes. Take mental note of which color combinations are pleasing to you. I highly recommend keeping a page or two in your sketchbook for palette swatches.

Beautiful color combinations are present all around us. When I'm out for a walk or on any sort of adventure, I like to take photos of the pleasing color palettes I encounter. The guidelines to color theory that we will cover in this chapter will assist you in selecting and implementing the perfect colors in your drawings!

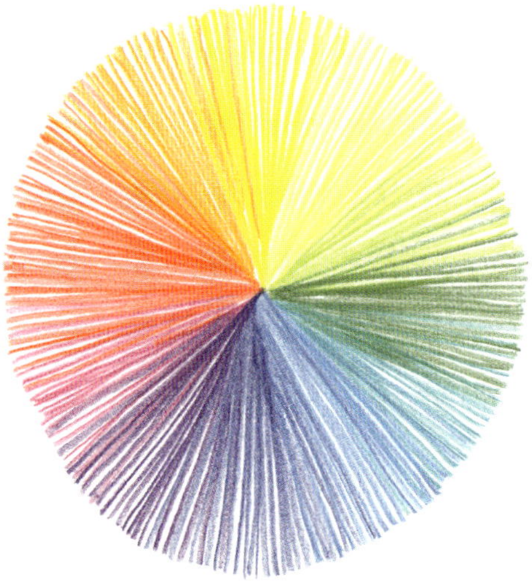

It may be tempting to incorporate as many colors as possible into your piece, but limiting your color palette to no more than five colored pencil colors will create a cleaner, more cohesive piece.

COMPLEMENTARY COLORS

Complementary colors are opposite one another on the color wheel. Some examples of complementary colors are blue and orange, yellow and purple, and red and green. If you were to combine these two colors, they would create a neutral. Complementary colors are quite striking when used together in an image.

If you are using complementary colors in a drawing, I recommend having your drawing be predominantly one color with pops of color added by its complement. For instance, a primarily blue underwater scene might be accented by some small, orange goldfish.

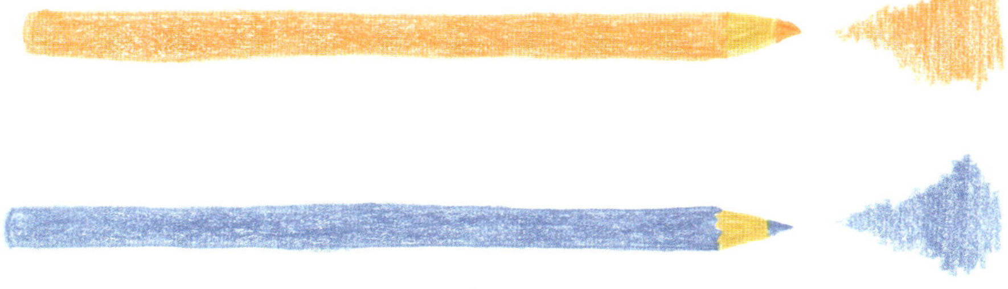

ANALOGOUS COLORS

Analogous colors are next to one another on the color wheel. An example of these is yellow, yellow-green, and green. Analogous colors create instant harmony in an image and are pretty fail-safe.

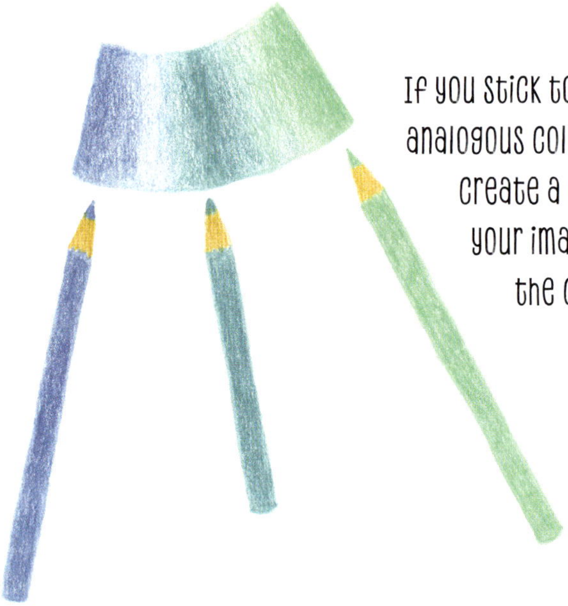

If you stick to a specific selection of analogous colors in your drawing, it can create a strong sense of mood in your image depending on whether the colors are warm or cool.

WARM VS. COOL COLORS

The color wheel is evenly split between warm and cool colors. Warm colors create an energizing and uplifting feel, while cool colors lend a calmer and perhaps more mysterious mood. Have you noticed that you used certain colors when decorating your home to create a certain mood in a room? Look at the examples of warm and cool colors, and see what kinds of emotions come up for you!

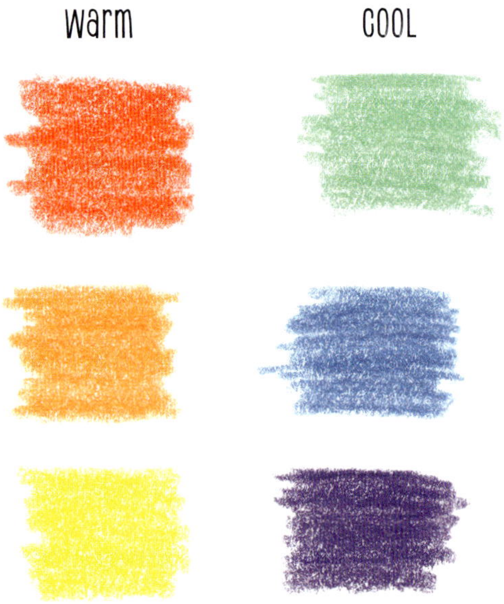

NEUTRALS

Neutrals are some of my favorite colors to use in my drawings because they go with everything! Neutrals generally consist of browns and grays as well as black and white.

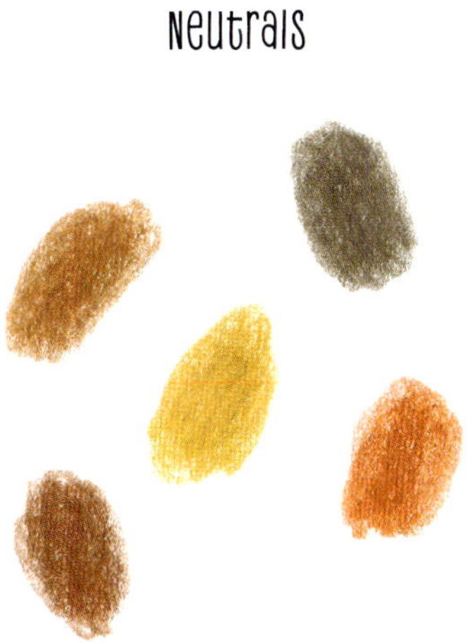

When I feel like I'm going overboard with bright colors in a drawing or my color palette has become too varied, I typically switch to using neutral colors for the rest of the image to avoid a visually confusing final drawing.

LAYERING TO CREATE NEW COLORS

As you know, colored pencils do not blend; instead, you layer them on top of one another to create a new color. By doing this, you can essentially create any color you desire even if you don't have it in your colored pencil set. Remember to always start with the lighter color, and then add the darker one on top for better control.

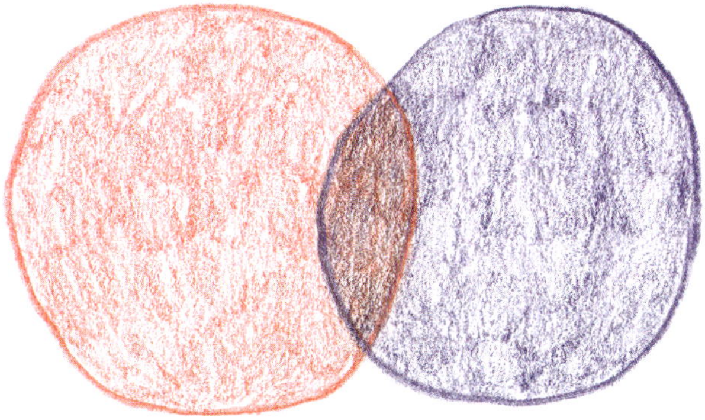

Visualize your color palette before you start drawing, and combine theory with what you know and feel instinctively when it comes to implementing colors in your drawings.

CREATING ART ON THE GO

Now that we've covered tools and materials, drawing techniques, and color theory, it's time to grab our gear and use our newfound skills to make some art while out and about! A change of scenery can trigger a lot of inspiration, even if that means just going for a walk to your neighborhood park or coffee shop.

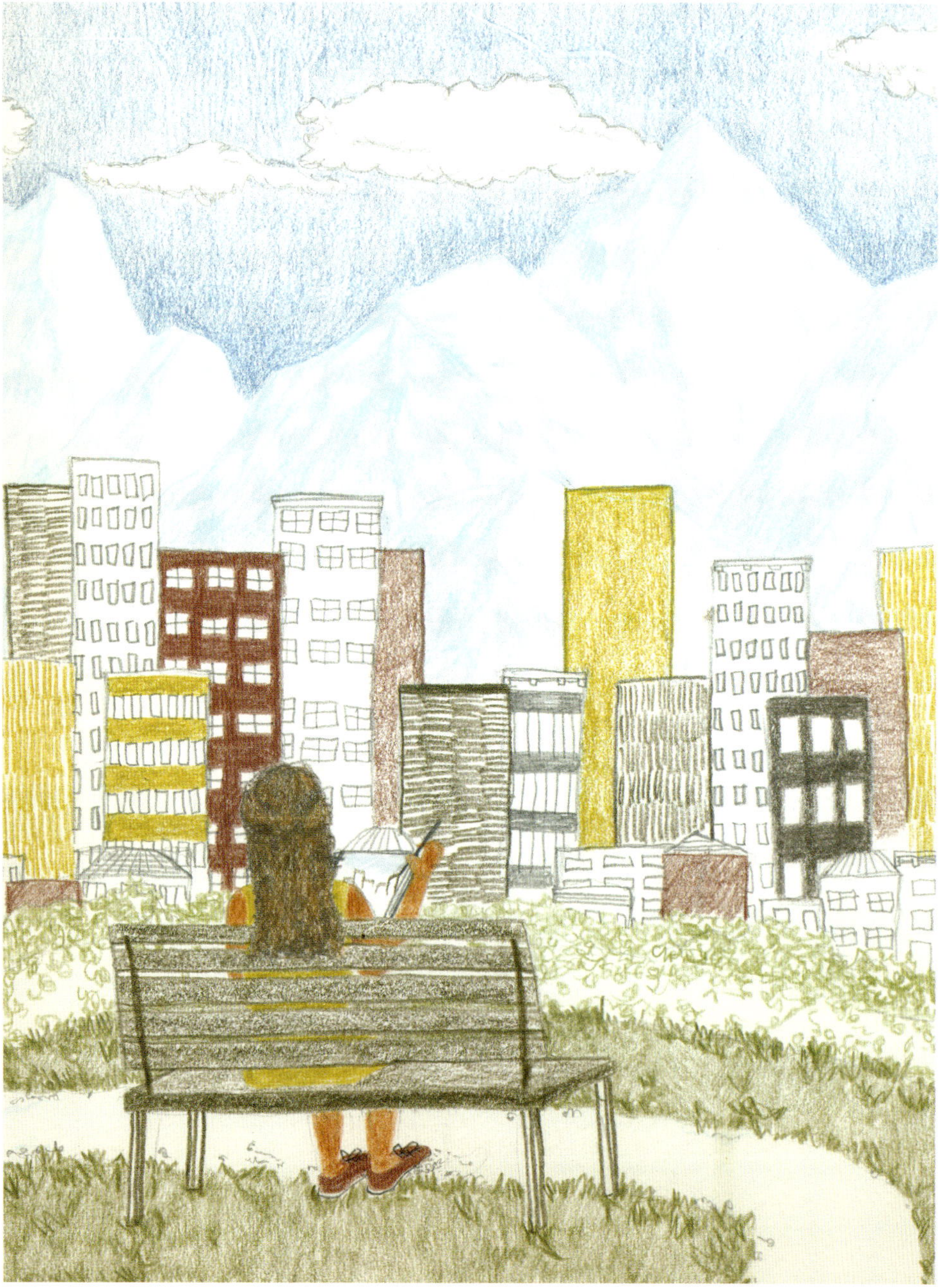

TRAVEL COMPANION: A SKETCHBOOK

If possible, bring your sketchbook with you wherever you go. You never know when inspiration may strike! Carrying your sketchbook is a powerful reminder to keep a keen eye for interesting people, places, and things. You may notice yourself being even more observant of the world around you. Inspiration can arise in any situation—from standing in line at the grocery store, to taking a walk around the block, to viewing a beautiful, new landscape while traveling. Keep in mind that you will want to choose a sketchbook that can fit into your bag for portability.

A PENCIL CASE FULL OF GOODNESS

It's time to load up your pencil case with all of your necessities before heading out on your adventure. When selecting which colored pencils to take with you, refer to your knowledge of color theory (see "Color Theory Basics" on page 18), and try to keep a refined selection of colors. Something I've learned as an artist is that it is much easier to make a lovely, cohesive artwork with a limited color palette than it is to try and incorporate the extensive range of colors found in a colored pencil set.

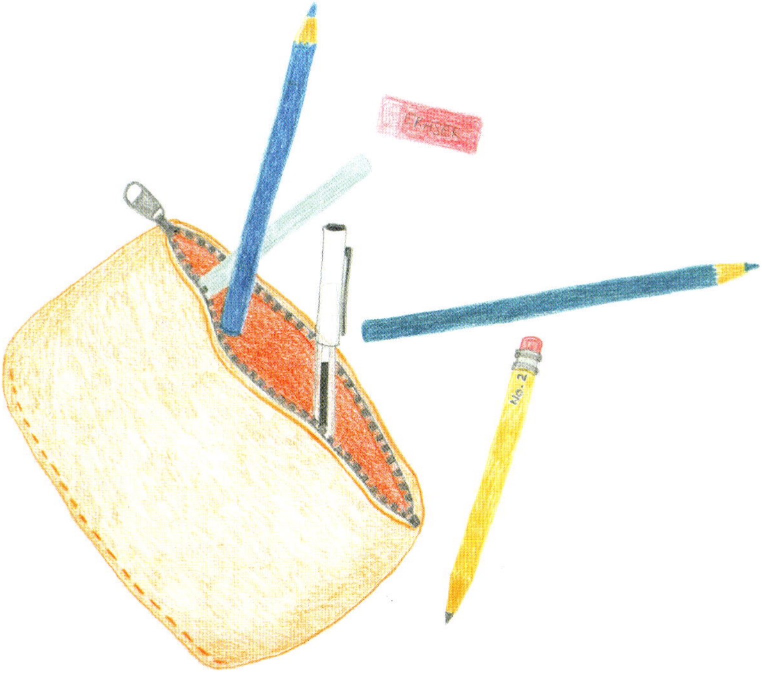

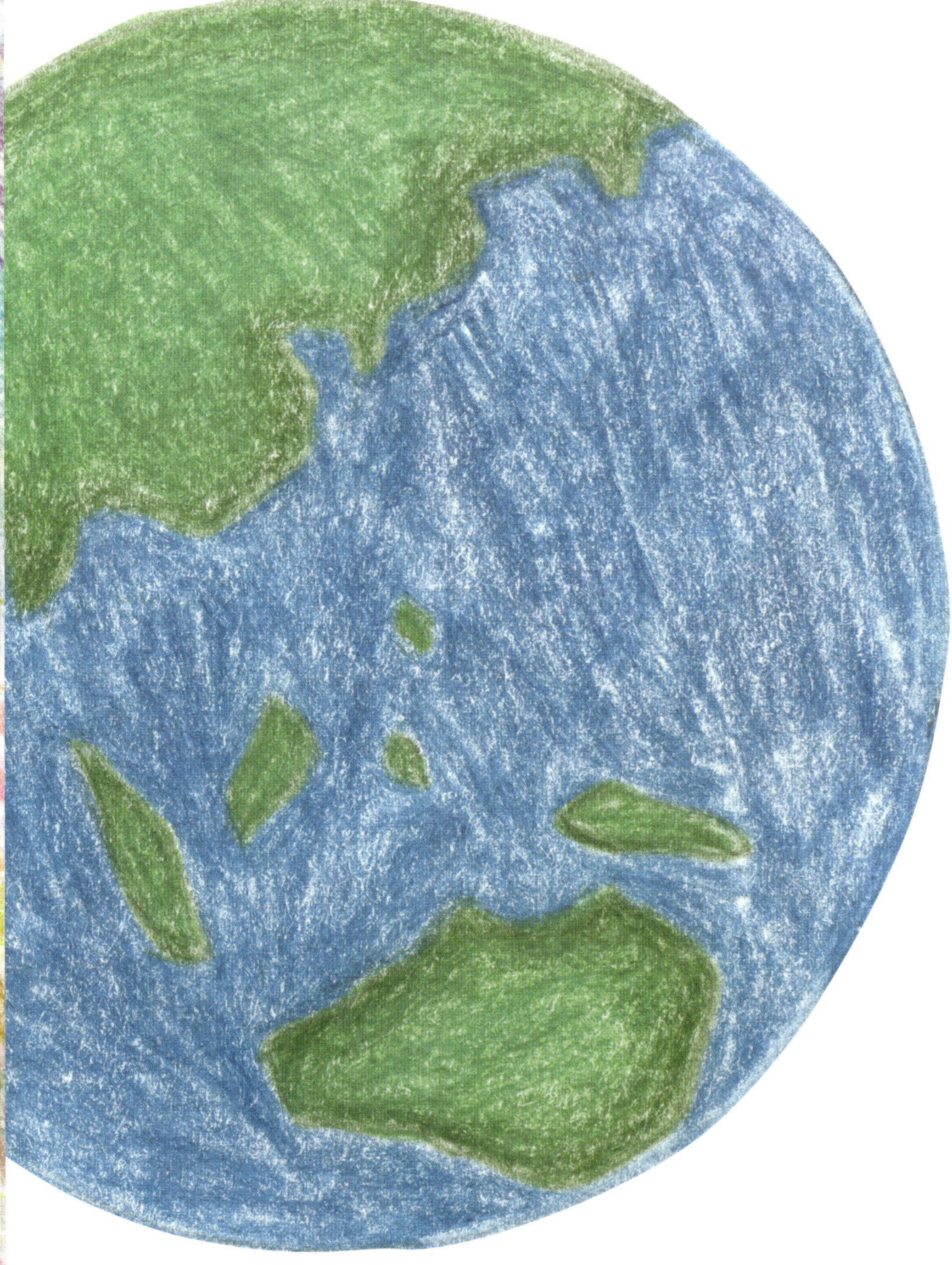

Once you feel comfortable drawing while out and about, it will feel like the world is your oyster—you can draw anything, anywhere!

PACKING UP SUPPLIES FOR PORTABILITY

I find it's easy to get carried away when packing up my art supplies. Sometimes it seems like I pack my entire art-supply collection into my backpack! Not only is this (literally) a pain to carry around, but I also find that I have less direction and get more easily side-tracked when I bring too many options for art supplies and paper. As the old adage goes, less is more!

To start, I choose a small backpack or satchel to hold my supplies. This way, I am limited by space in terms of how many supplies I can bring with me. If I'm feeling ambitious, I bring my whole set of colored pencils with me, but sometimes it can be even more effective to select three to five colored pencils in a single color palette and bring only those. This will force you to create artwork with a cohesive color palette. Also, don't forget your sharpener and eraser! Additional helpful supplies include a graphite pencil and ink pen. I generally put all of these materials into a pencil case to protect them.

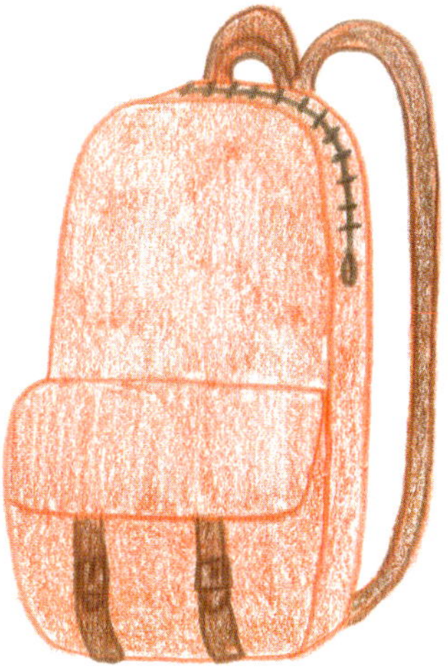

Finally, don't forget your paper! For me, this usually means a sketchpad or notebook of some sort. If you plan to create artwork to show or share, it's best to bring higher-quality paper. (See page 8 for tips on selecting the right kind of paper for you.)

Consider bringing a sweater or jacket, depending on the weather. Often, I'll go out walking and feel fine without a sweater, but after sitting still and drawing for a long period of time, I'll start to feel a bit chilly!

MY FAVORITE PLACES TO DRAW

I almost always prefer drawing while I'm on the go. If I spend too much time drawing at home, I get serious cabin fever! Plus, there are so many different things to see and experience when you change your scenery. This change in stimuli can lead to amazing inspiration! Some of my favorite places to draw are at cafés, in the park, and in museums.

Colored pencils aren't messy and they require few tools, making them perfect for on-the-go drawing.

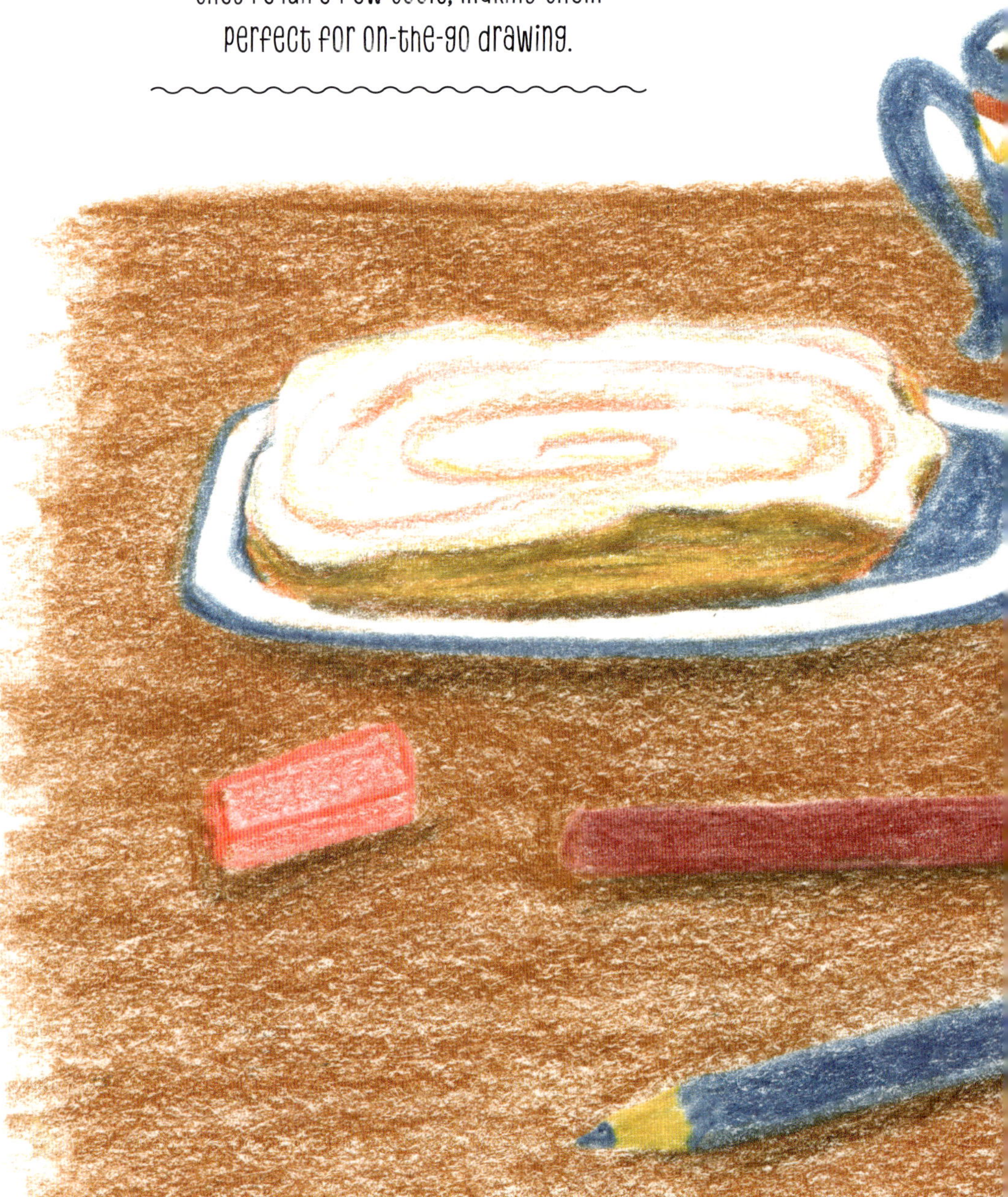

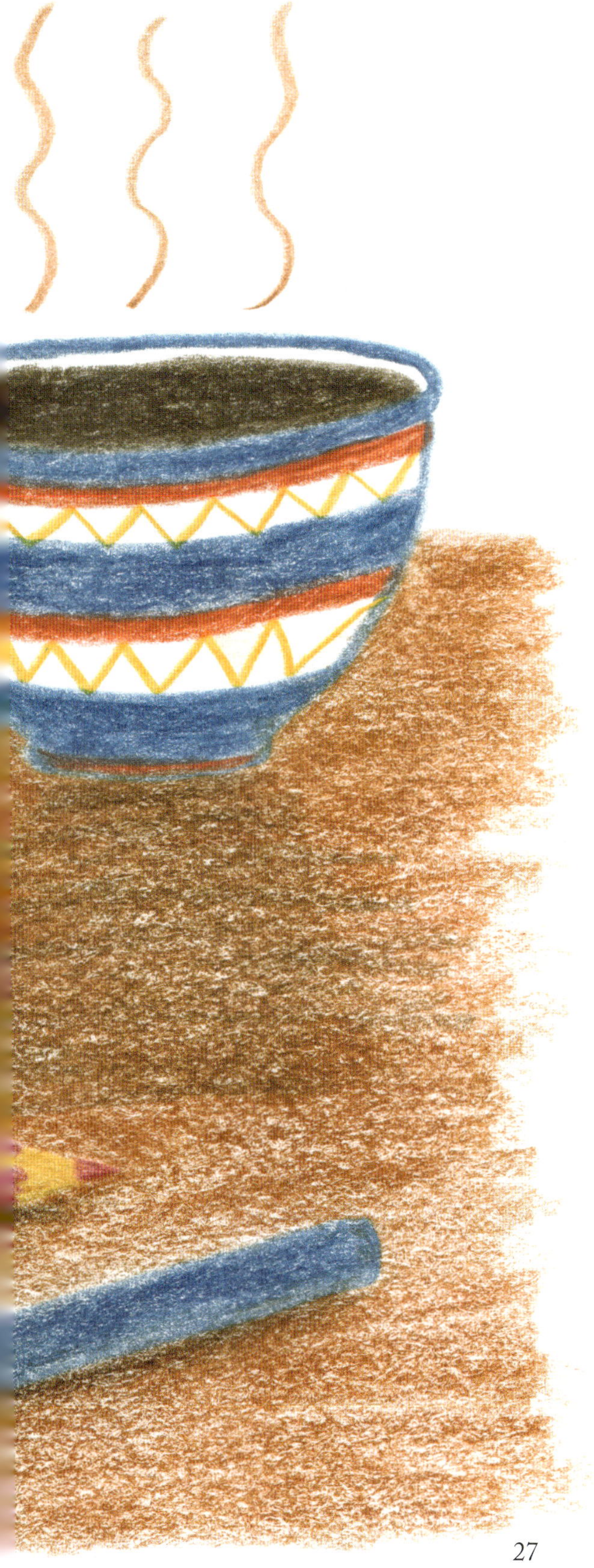

COFFEE + ART

My all-time favorite space to draw in is a café or coffee shop. Fortunately, I live within walking distance of a number of cafés, but even while traveling, I make it a point to seek out the area's coffee shops. There's something about a coffee shop that has such a welcoming and warm energy. You can really get a sense of an area's culture by its cafés!

Coffee shops are also great for people-watching. I love the feeling of being in the energy of others (while also getting a nice boost from my cup of coffee!), and I find I can create so much artwork in this setting.

PARKS ARE PERFECT

A park is also an amazing place to gather inspiration; sunshine, a fresh breeze, and natural surroundings can do wonders for your creativity! Also, parks are great for people—and animal—watching. Sitting at a park bench or picnic table, you can examine and capture the movement of nature while also getting some vitamin D!

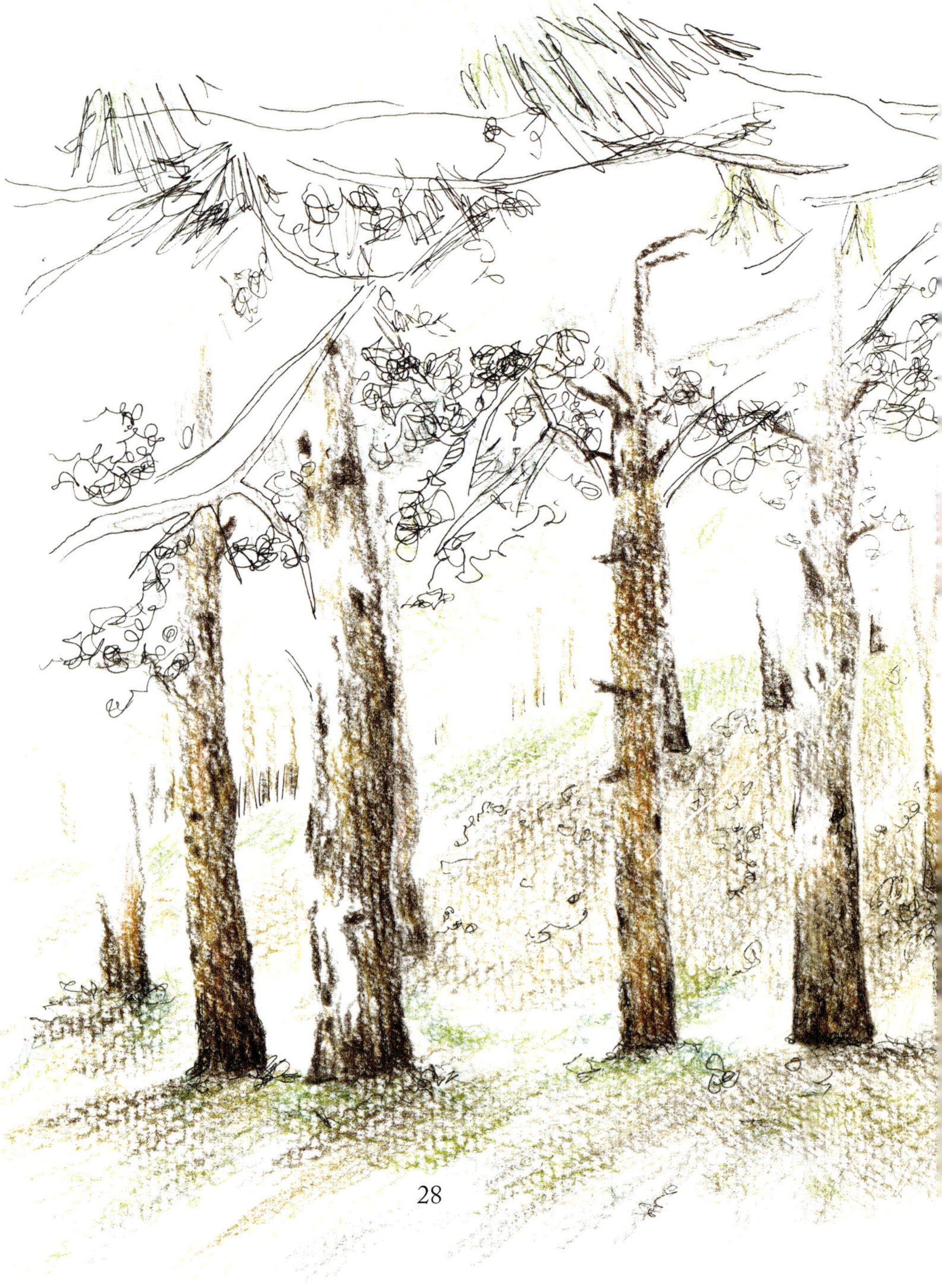

MAKE IT A MUSEUM DAY

A museum is a great place to draw because it gives you the opportunity to draw from other people's inspiration. If you go to a history museum, you can practice your colored-pencil skills by drawing some of the exhibits! At an art museum, take some time to wander around and soak up the inspiration from the masters—historical and contemporary! Similar to parks and cafés, museums offer a great opportunity for people-watching.

Next time you're at a museum, practice drawing people in natural positions, such as sitting, standing, and walking.

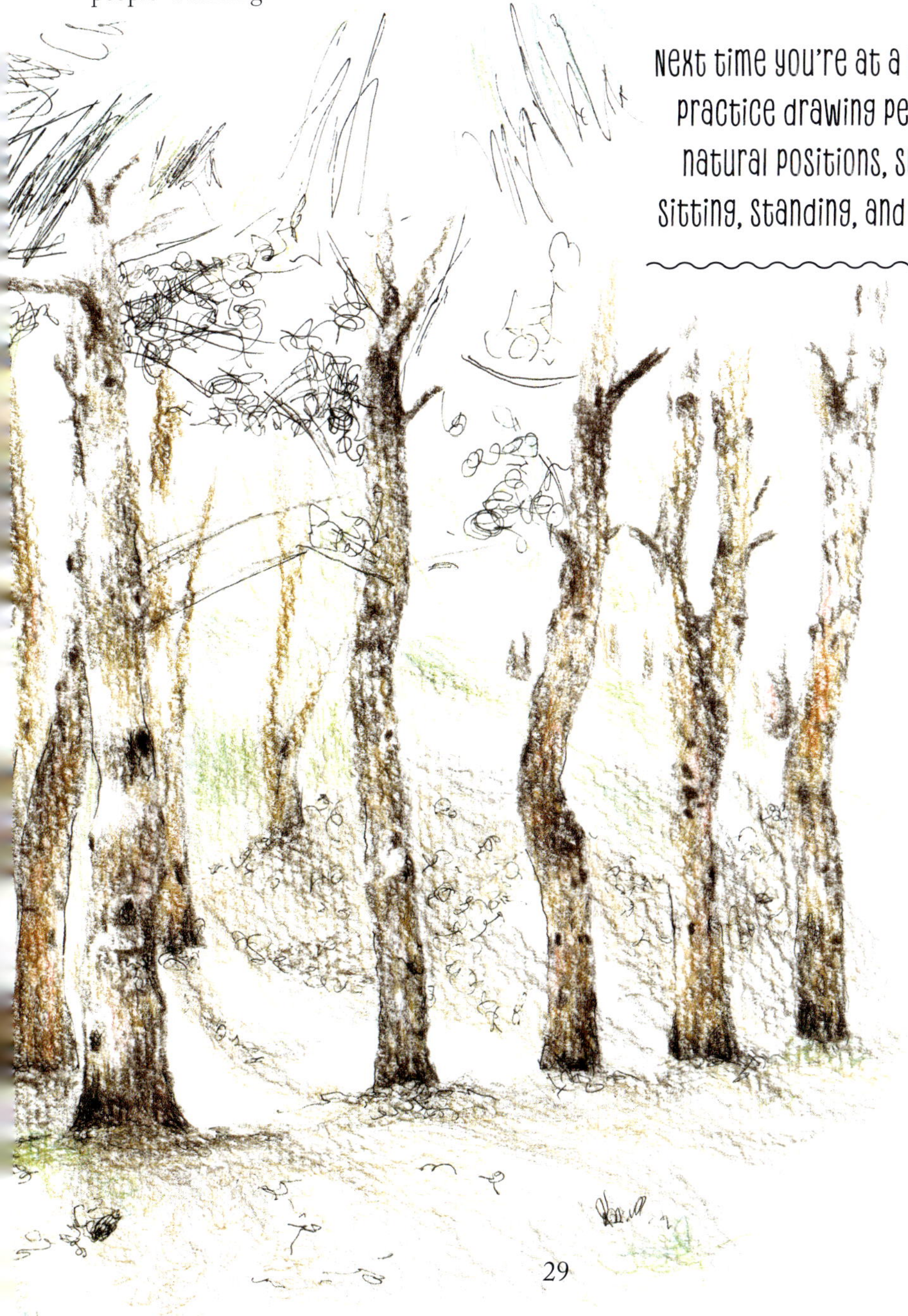

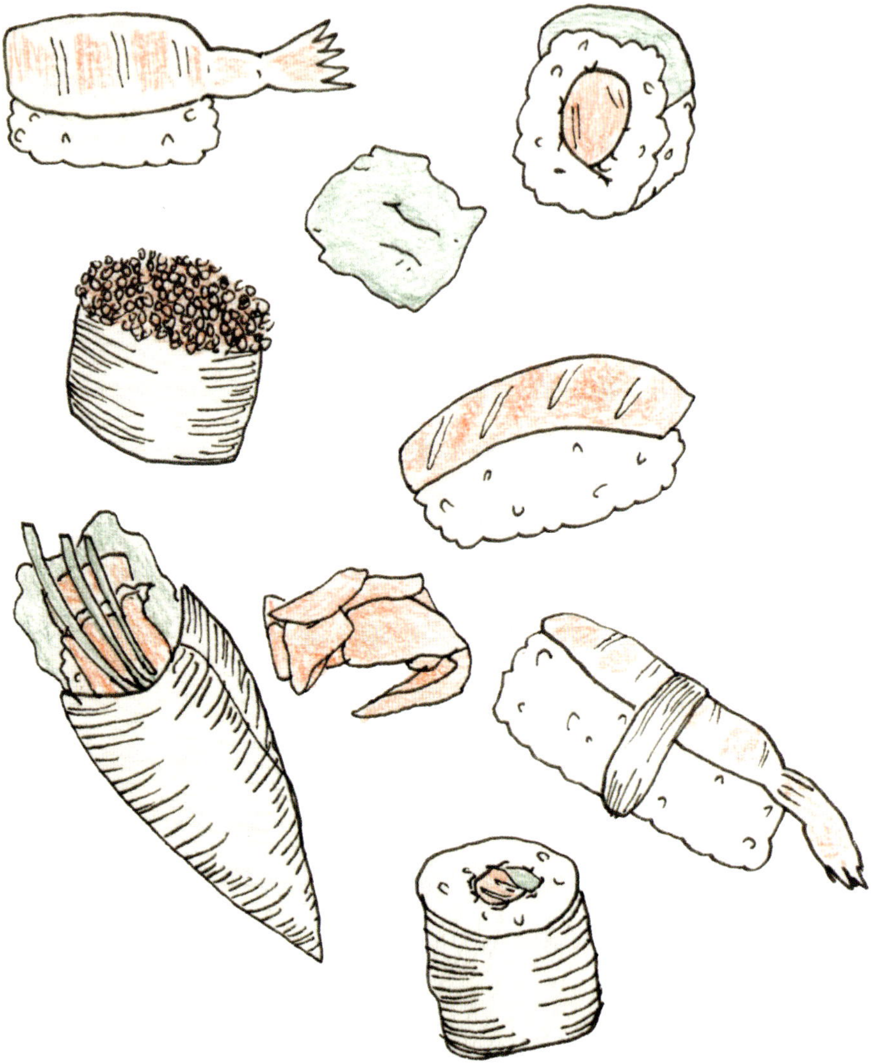

What's your favorite restaurant? Similar to a coffee shop, a casual restaurant is a great place to sit and draw. Try drawing your food, or maybe there's a beautiful, colorful garnish that would make a quick drawing subject. If you're a sushi fan, draw a few of the pieces you've ordered. The good news is they won't get cold before you eat them if your drawing ends up taking longer than you'd planned!

LET'S START DRAWING!

Now it's time to head out and create. Try to draw as much as you can. Don't worry if you aren't feeling creative or inspired. You can always draw the things around you. You can even pull all of the belongings out of your bag and draw them.

Drawing outside and in new scenery is not only exciting, it's also a great way to improve as an artist! Pushing yourself out of your comfort zone allows you to make mistakes, and from these mistakes we often grow as artists. In fact, there may be times when you look at your "mistake" and realize you like the look of it and can incorporate this into your personal drawing style! Channel the energy from the scene you are in—this will make for lively and emotionally charged artwork.

If you don't have time to sit and make a complete artwork while you are on the go, take a minute or two to render a quick sketch of the scene and jot down a few descriptive words about the setting. Sometimes it can be helpful to snap a couple of photos to reference later. With this information, you can complete your artwork at home.

I carry my sketchbook with me just about anywhere I go. It's comforting to know that I have the tools at hand to make a drawing whenever I am struck by a moment of inspiration. I find that drawing while I'm on the go helps me to be more mindful and grateful for my experiences. What a wonderful thing it is to flip through an old sketchbook and be transported back to a previous time, place, and feeling!

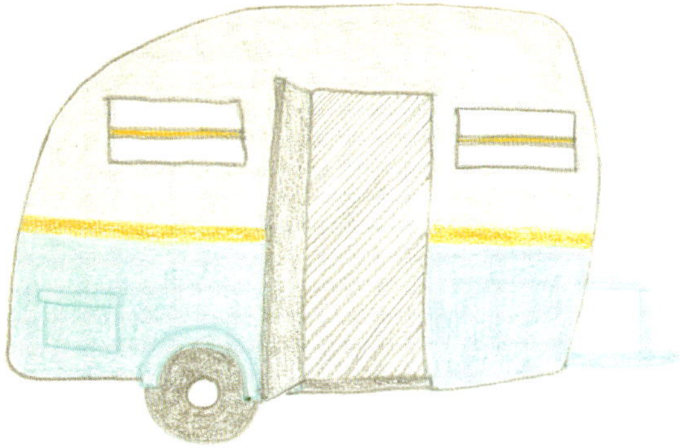

It is often helpful to get your hands moving. Warming up with a seemingly mundane and easy drawing can get your creative juices flowing.

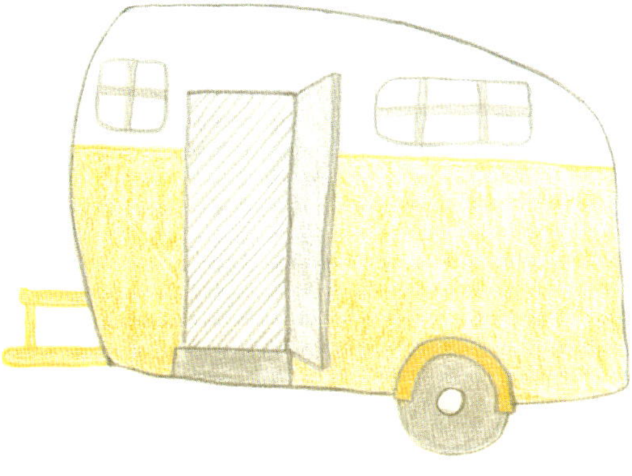

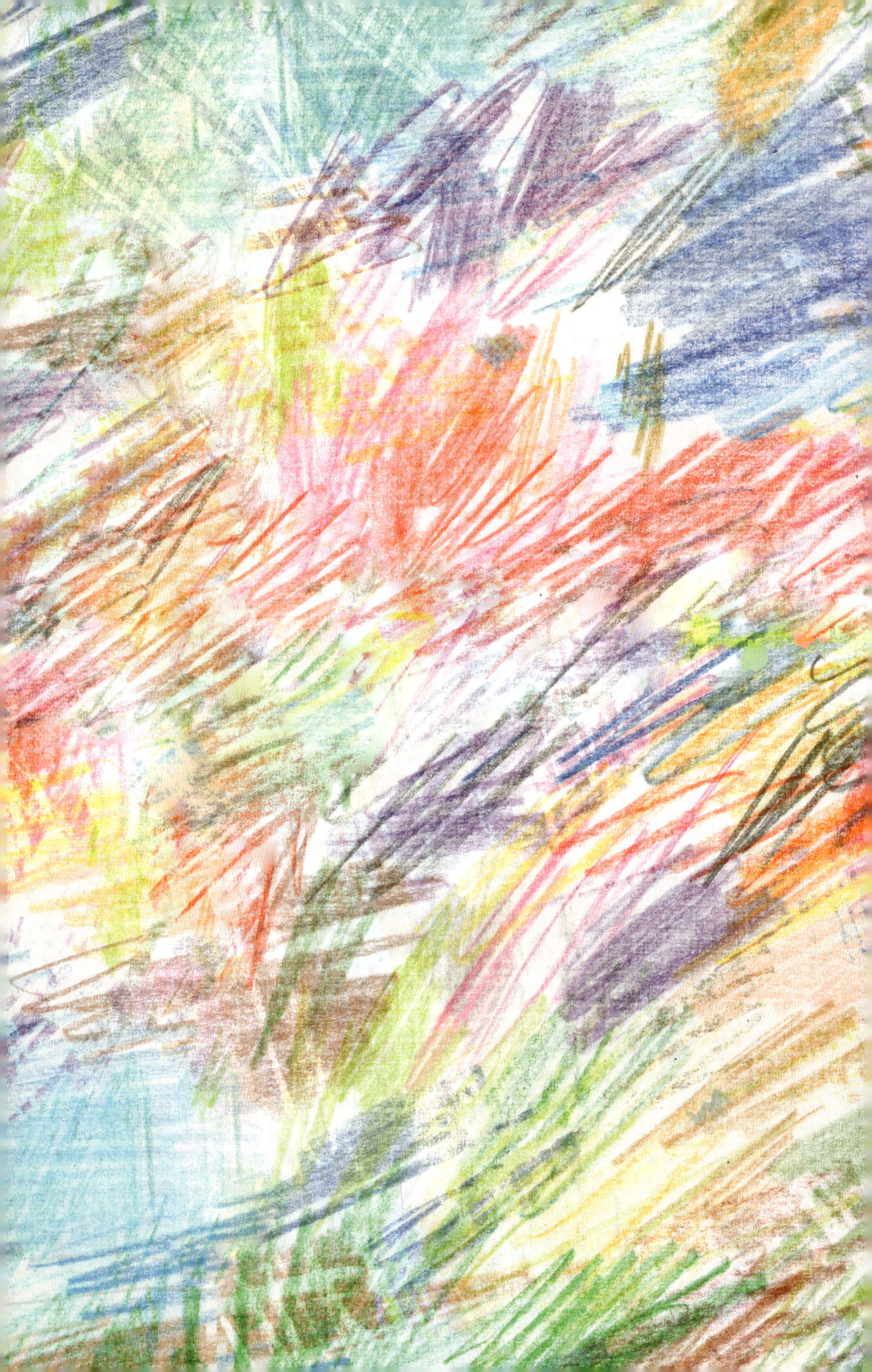

STEP-BY-STEP DRAWING EXERCISES

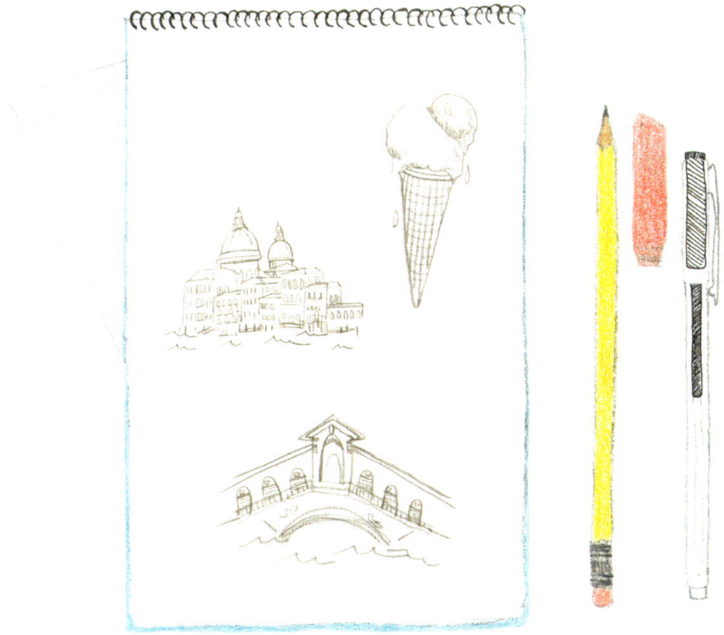

INTERIOR DECORATING

Even though I love plants and find that greenery can really lift my mood, I am not a natural gardener. While my real-life cacti and herbs rarely make it past a few months, my illustrated plants keep their liveliness forever! My favorite plants at present are *Monstera deliciosa* and any kind of succulent. Both present such interesting forms to capture in artwork. Another exciting part of drawing plants is that you get to choose the planter pot and stand of your dreams! There are no limits or price tags. Design a plant arrangement that suits your greenery dreams.

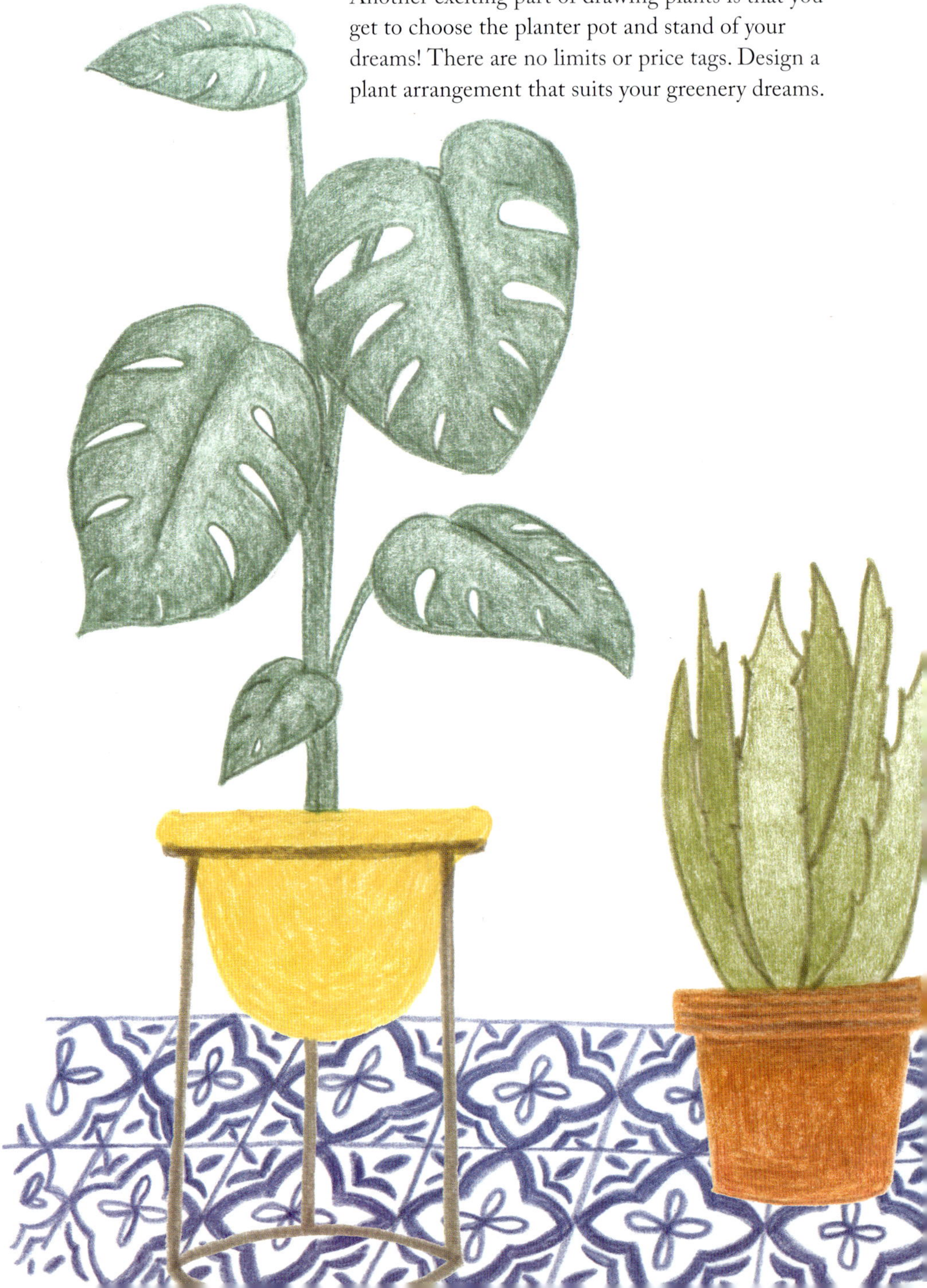

You may have noticed that a lot of flower pots are terra-cotta colored. Terra-cotta has a reddish color that is harmonious with all green plant life because it is green's complementary color (see "Color Theory Basics" on page 18).

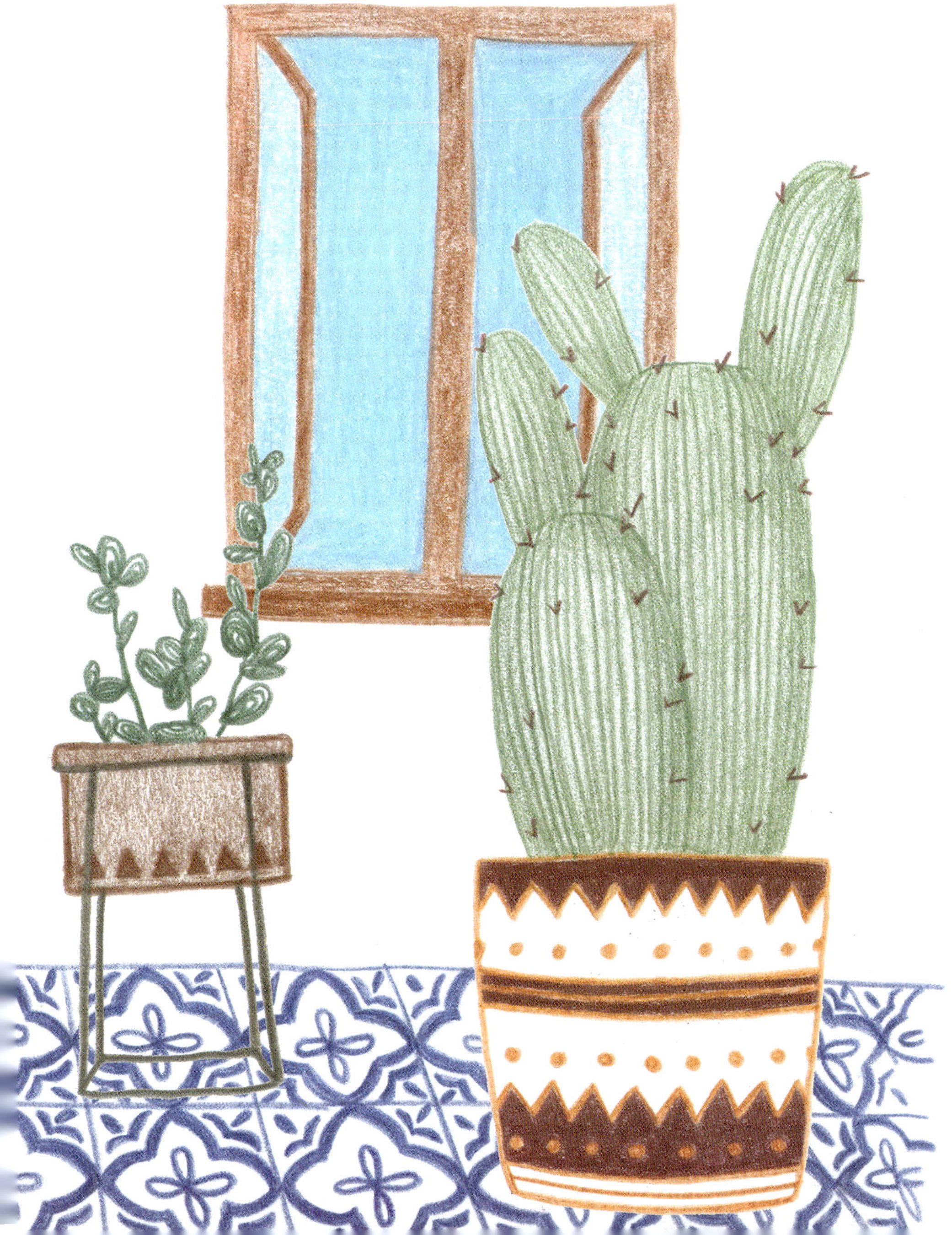

CACTUS

Cacti and other succulents are fun to draw because they present a stiffer and often simpler shape than more intricate and tangled plants, such as common herbs and many flowers.

STEP 1

For this quirky little cactus, start off by outlining the pot and cactus with the colors you chose for both. For the cactus, use connecting oval shapes.

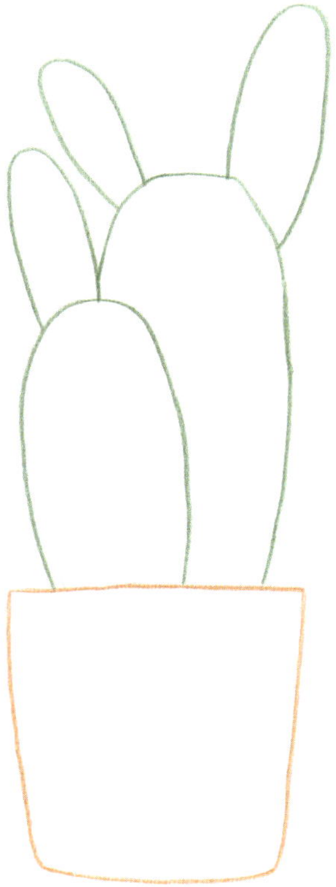

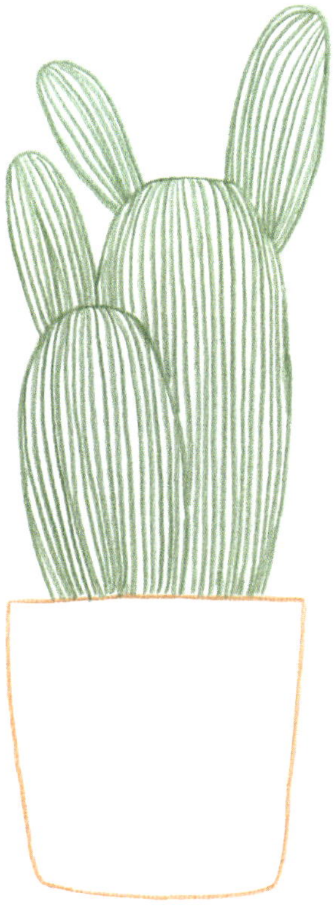

STEP 2

Fill in the cactus with green lines mimicking the curves of the ovals.

STEP 3

Shade in the ovals, and make the green darker near the edges of the ovals as well as where the ovals connect.

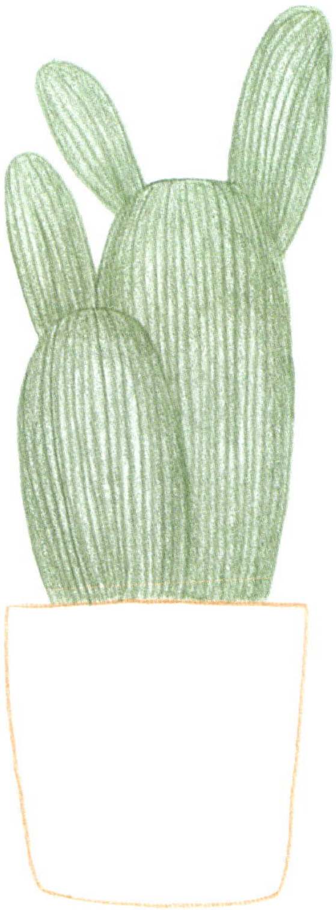

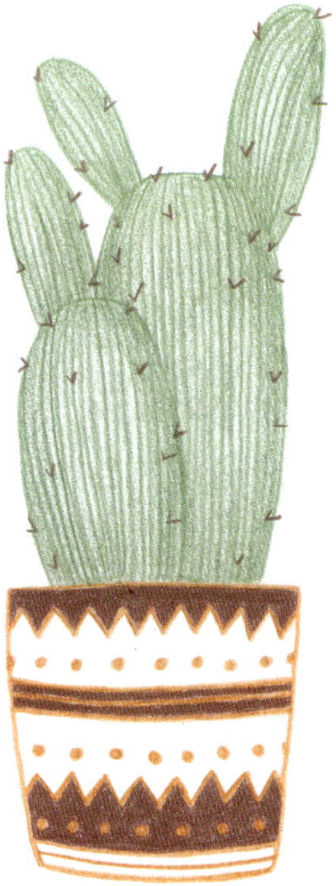

STEP 4

On a separate piece of paper, test out some sample patterns for the pot. Which one do you like the best? Copy that pattern onto your pot. I used the deep red color from the pot to make the pricks on the cactus!

MONSTERA DELICIOSA

Monstera deliciosa is commonly referred to as the "Swiss cheese plant" because of all the holes caused by splits in the leaves.

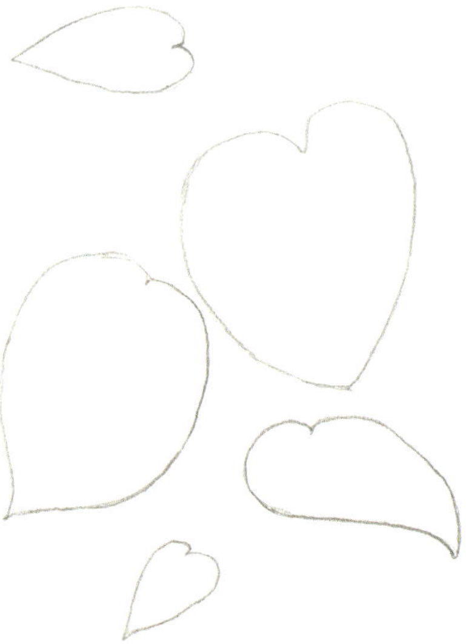

STEP 1

Monstera deliciosa leaves look heart-shaped. To start, outline the leaves of the plant, excluding the slits and holes, by drawing a bunch of hearts at different positions and heights.

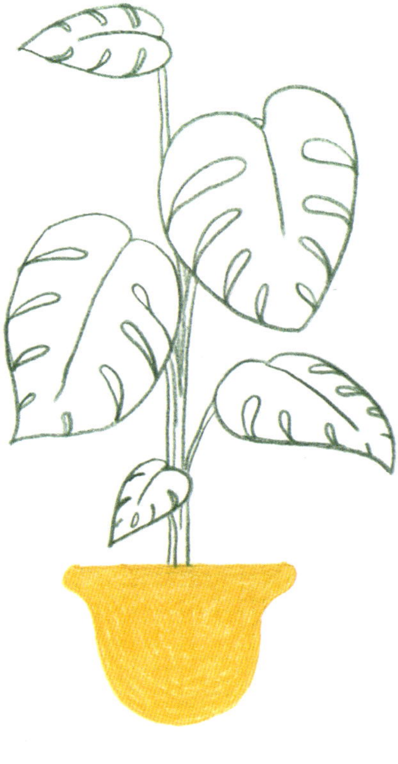

STEP 2

Next, draw the slits in the leaves by creating looplike shapes beginning at the edge of the leaf and moving slightly back toward the stem. Draw stems from the leaves. Connect them at the bottom where your pot will start. Then pick a color that sparks your inspiration, draw a simple pot shape, and fill it in.

STEP 3

For this planter, I went for a mid-century style. Choose a neutral color to draw the stand for the pot. First, draw an oval on the floor and then a line under the lip of the pot. Connect these two segments with three straight lines.

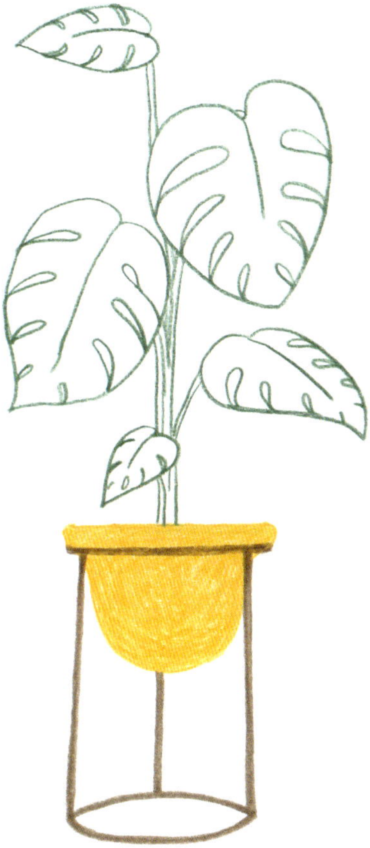

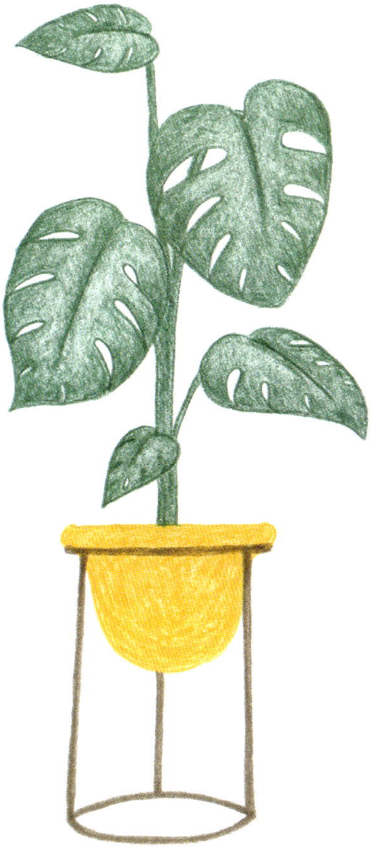

STEP 4

Lastly, shade in the leaves with the same color you used to outline them. Use a heavier hand to shade near the stem and the outline of the leaf, and use lighter shading in between. Do not shade in the slits.

ADDING A BACKGROUND

Right now, our plants are floating around on our paper. Let's ground them by adding a background to create a scene.

STEP 1

When "planting" your plant in a room, it is important to first indicate where the wall meets the floor. Draw a line somewhere between the lower oval of your plant stand and the bottom of your pot.

STEP 2

I like the way blue looks with mustard yellow, so I added a blue carpet. To draw carpet, create a weave-like pattern by adding arrow shapes, with each row reversing direction.

STEP 3

Hardwood floors are my favorite, so I added a warm chestnut color to indicate wood floors under the carpet. Since the pot and carpet are quite striking in their colors, I chose a neutral color for the wall.

Consider dedicating a page or two in your sketchbook to different kinds of leaves. This will be a great reference any time you're creating a scene with greenery and don't have plants in front of you to reference. If you're feeling daring, experiment with making some leaf shapes from your imagination.

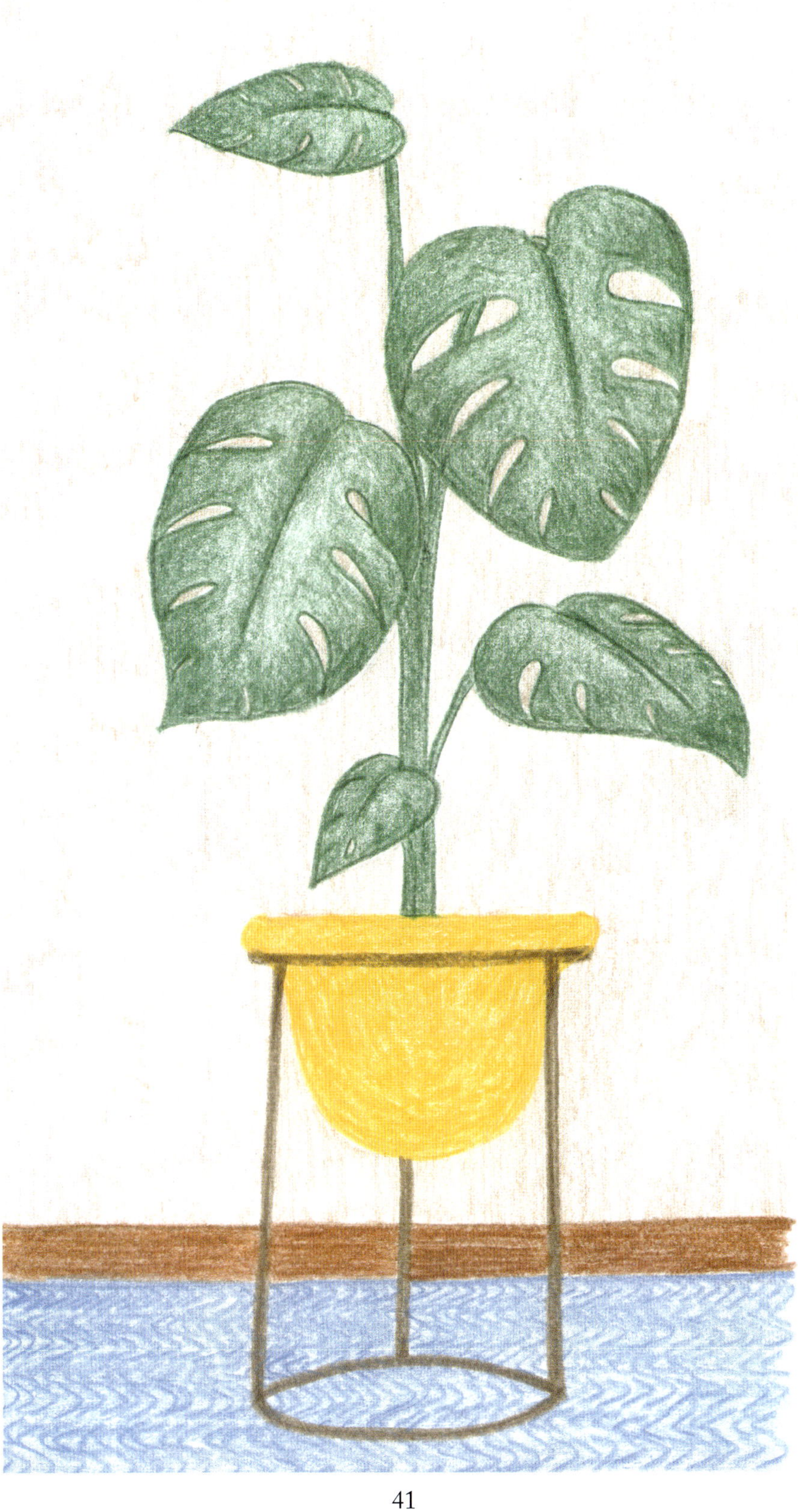

TILES

Here are some additional flooring options!

STEP 1

To create a room with a tile floor, first draw a line where the floor would meet the wall.

STEP 2

Next, starting at the center of the line already drawn, draw perpendicular lines that extend toward the bottom of the page.

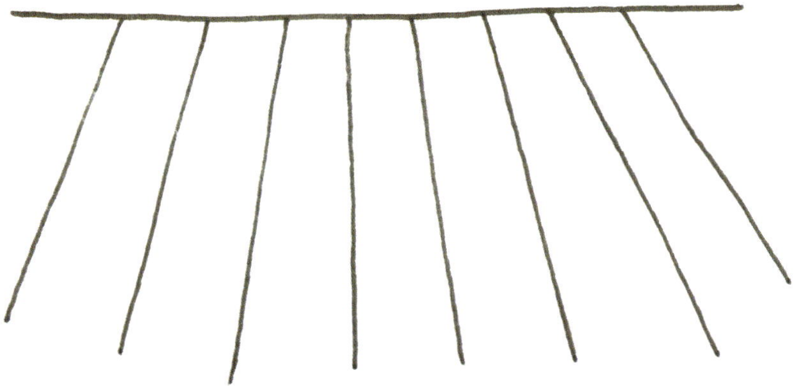

STEP 3

Add horizontal lines parallel to where the floor meets the wall. The lines should get farther apart as you move toward the bottom of the page. You should now have a gridlike pattern in perspective!

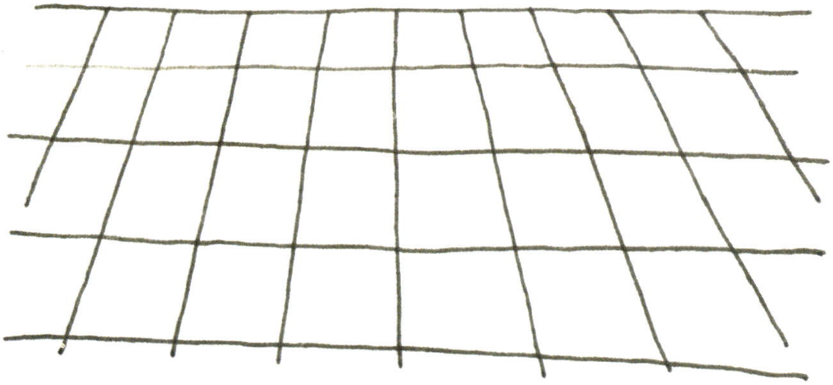

PATTERNS AND COLOR

Here is where things start to get more personalized. On scrap paper or in the designated patterns section of your sketchbook, draw some sample tiles. Tiles often have symmetrical patterns. When you choose one you like, transfer that onto each of the squares in your grid. (Want to see my tiles installed? See pages 34–35.)

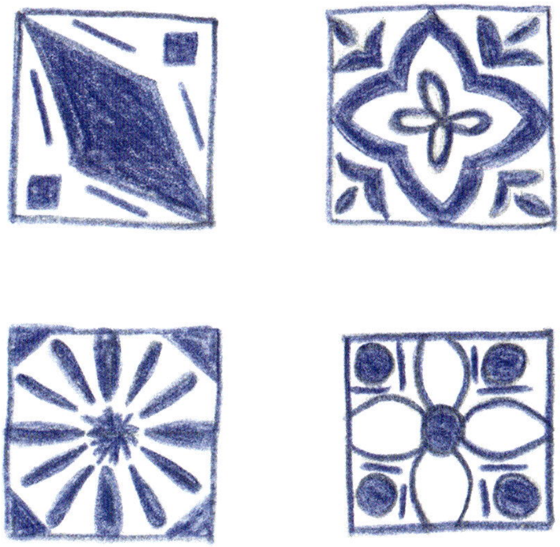

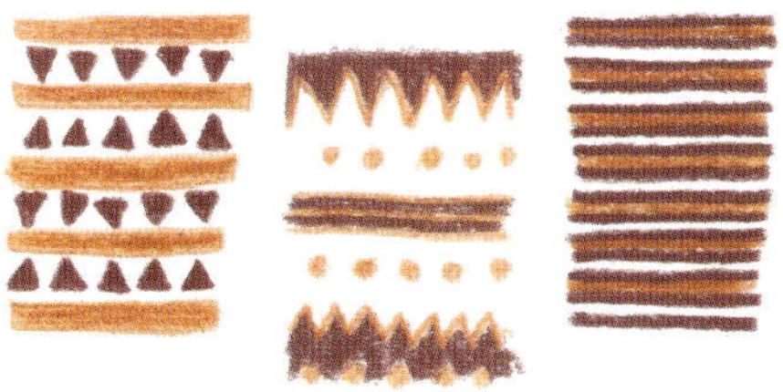

Hang on to your other patterns to use in future projects! I like to dedicate a section of my sketchbook to testing patterns, colors, and textures. It's helpful to have on hand, especially when I'm in a rut!

FRUITS & VEGGIES

Fruits and vegetables are not only delicious and healthy, they also make great subjects for your art! Fruits and vegetables all have their own colors, textures, and shapes, making them great for practicing drawing techniques and color theory.

Another wonderful thing about produce is that it's often readily available. You may even have some in your house right now—grab it if you do! Pay close attention to the details. Is the produce shiny, smooth, or rough? Does it have seeds? Are there stems or leaves? What colors are there? Close observation is key to differentiating fruits and veggies in your drawings.

Growing up, my mother always told me to eat my broccoli and packed an apple in my lunch every day. Not only did I grow to love eating fruits and veggies, but they've become commonplace in my drawings too!

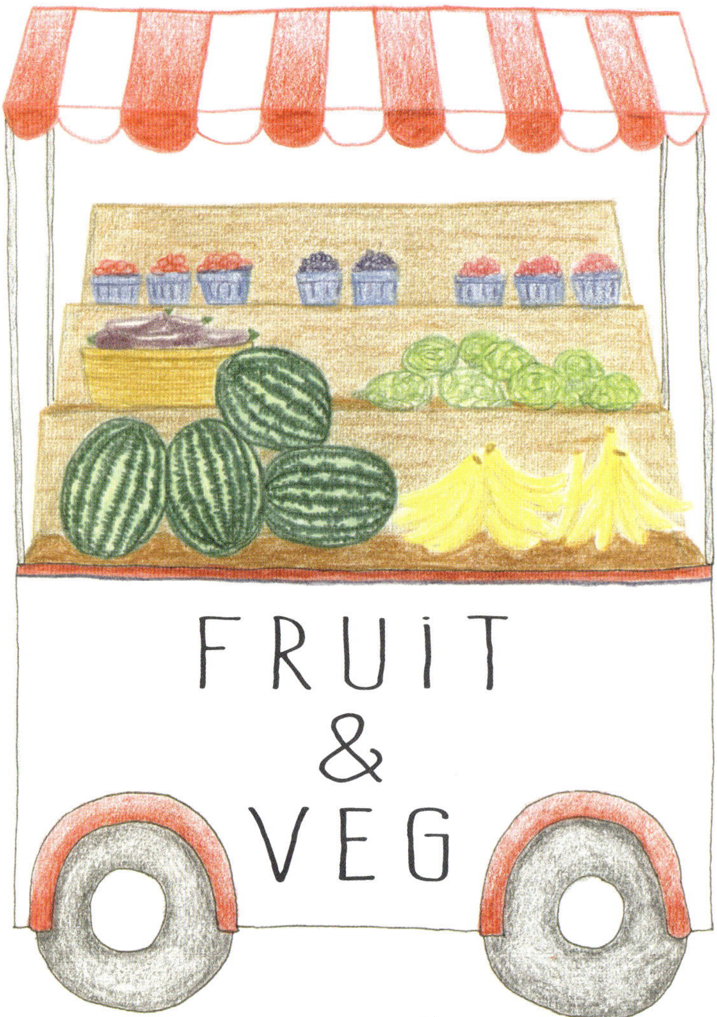

BROCCOLI

STEP 1

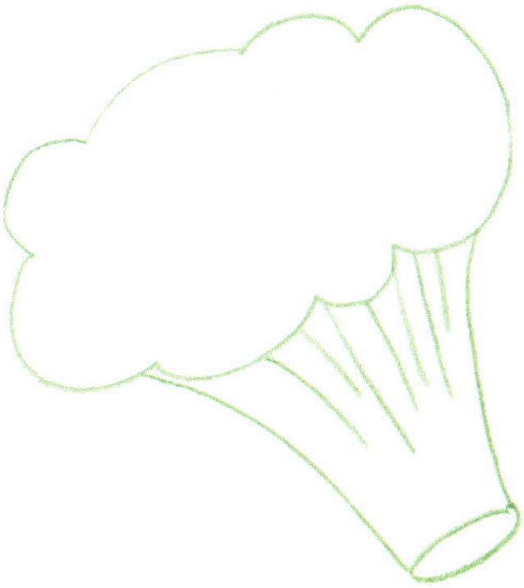

To start your broccoli drawing, first draw a cloud shape with a heavy contour line. This will be the bunch of florets at the end of the stalk. Then draw the stalk, and add in some extra lines for the different arms of the stalk.

When we were younger, my mother used to tell my brother and me that broccoli were like little trees. It's actually really helpful to think of them that way as you draw!

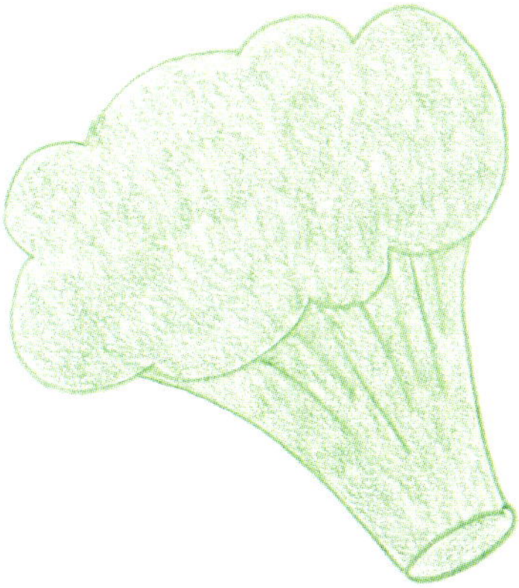

STEP 2

Next, using back-and-forth stroking, fill in the entire piece of broccoli with green.

STEP 3

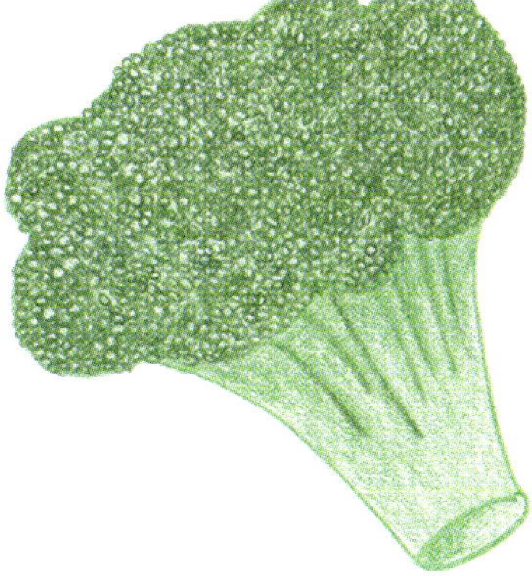

Now choose a darker green shade. With this color, draw many little circles for the florets. This creates a really cool textured effect! Add some shading under the florets to create dimension.

WHOLE WATERMELON

STEP 1

When starting your whole watermelon, first choose a dark, cool green colored pencil as well as a light greenish-yellow colored pencil. With the dark green, draw an oval with a little circle at the top. This is where the root attached to the melon.

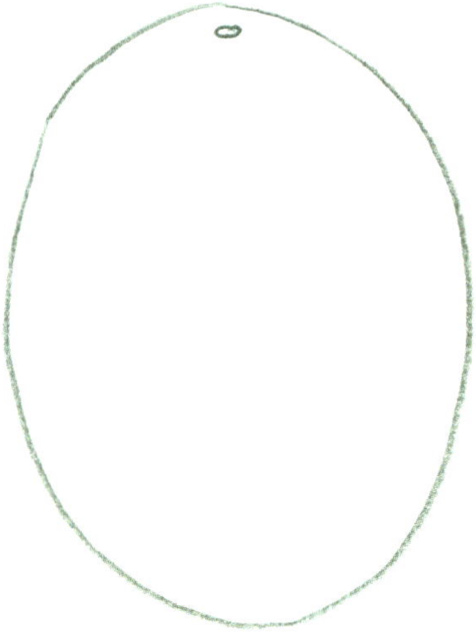

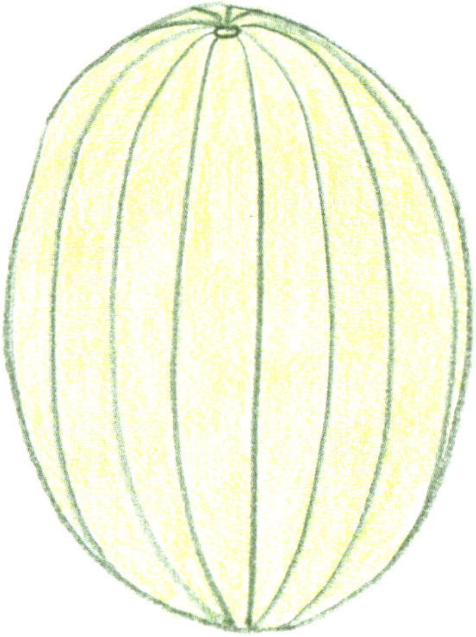

STEP 2

Next, color in the entire melon with the lighter shade, and then draw rounded curved lines with the darker green. These lines give the watermelon dimension and make it look spherical.

STEP 3

Finally, using the same dark green color, use the back-and-forth stroking technique roughly along the lines. There you have it—a juicy watermelon!

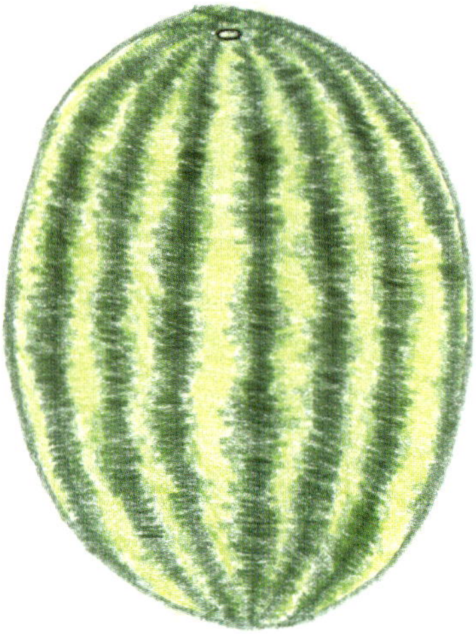

WATERMELON SLICE

STEP 1

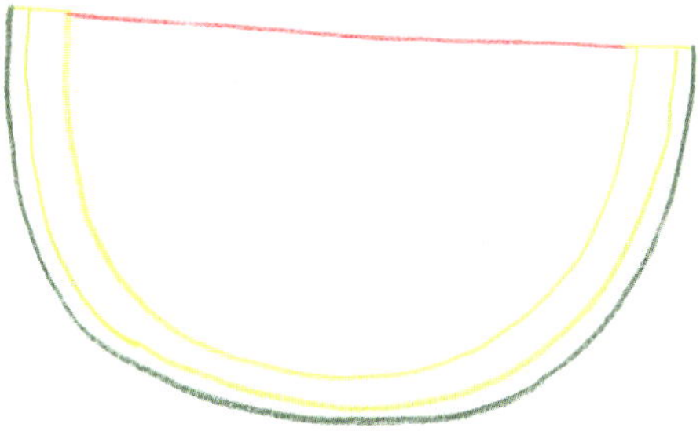

Use the same two green colors from the whole watermelon drawing, and grab a salmon or coral pink color for the deliciously sweet inside of your watermelon slice!

Draw three concentric half-circles: the outer one with dark green and the inner two with greenish-yellow. These lines indicate the rind. Then draw a straight line across these with pink.

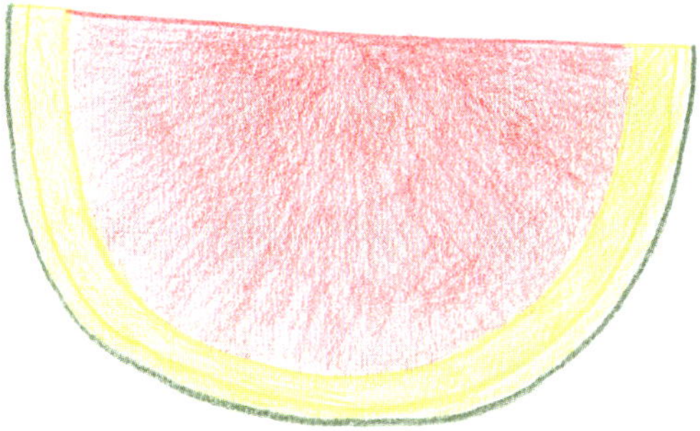

STEP 2

Fill in the rind with the greenish-yellow shade and the remainder of the slice with pink. I used back-and-forth stroking with the pink radiating out from the middle of the straight pink line.

STEP 3

Lastly, increase the saturation of the pink as it moves closer to the middle by layering with the same colored pencil. Grab your pen or a black colored pencil, and draw in the seeds.

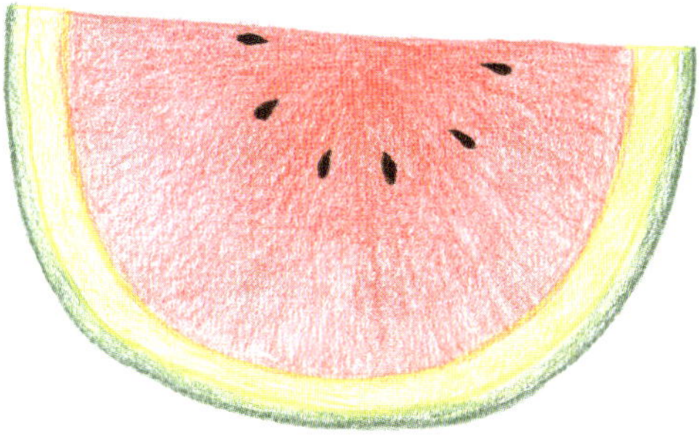

ARTICHOKE

STEP 1

Because the artichoke is a more complicated vegetable, I recommend starting your drawing by simply getting the general shape of the artichoke down with a regular pencil. Don't fuss with any detail at this point in your drawing.

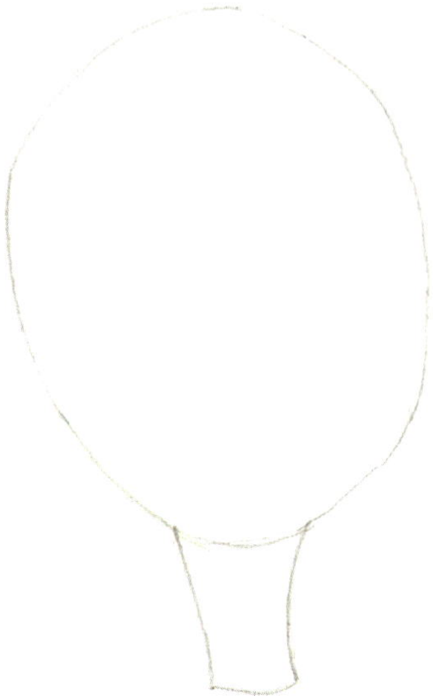

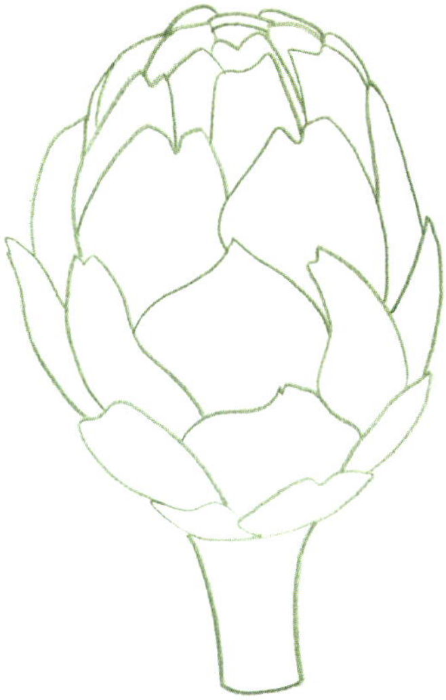

STEP 2

Now, choose three shades of green from your colored pencils. Include a light, medium, and dark shade of green. Using the darkest shade, contour the leaves and stem of the artichoke. This is a complicated vegetable and it helps a lot if you have one in front of you (or a photo reference)! Gently erase your initial graphite lines.

STEP 3

Next, use the light green to fill all of the leaves, and then use medium and dark greens to shade the stem.

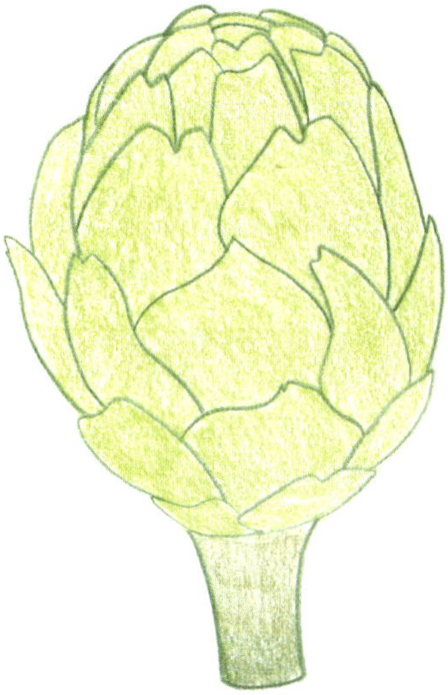

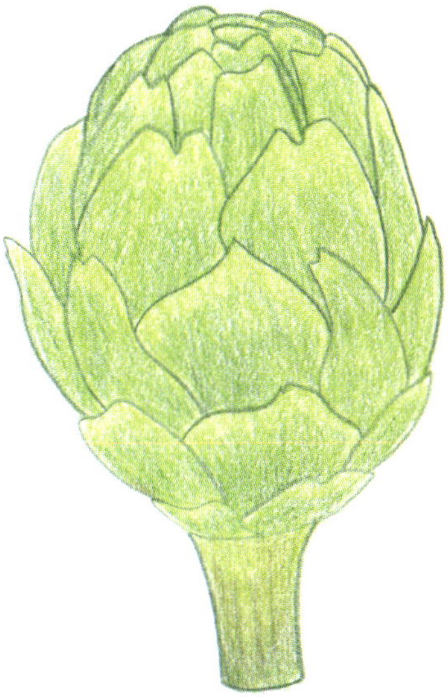

STEP 4

Using the medium green, layer on top of the light green and create a deeper color closer to where the leaf starts.

STEP 5

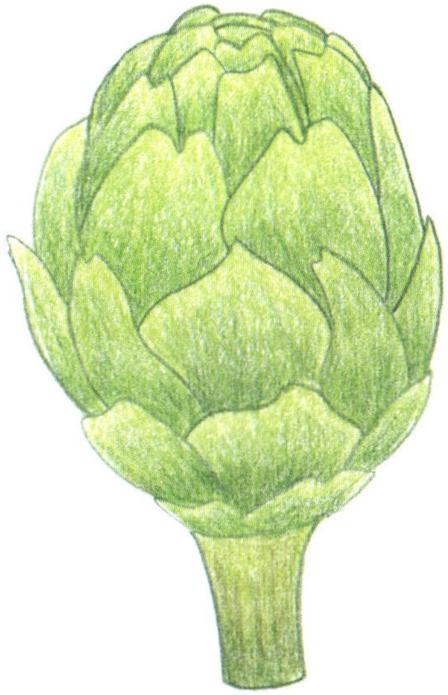

To create even more depth, use the dark green color to deepen the leaves near their bases.

This is a great vegetable with which to practice your shading!

EGGPLANT

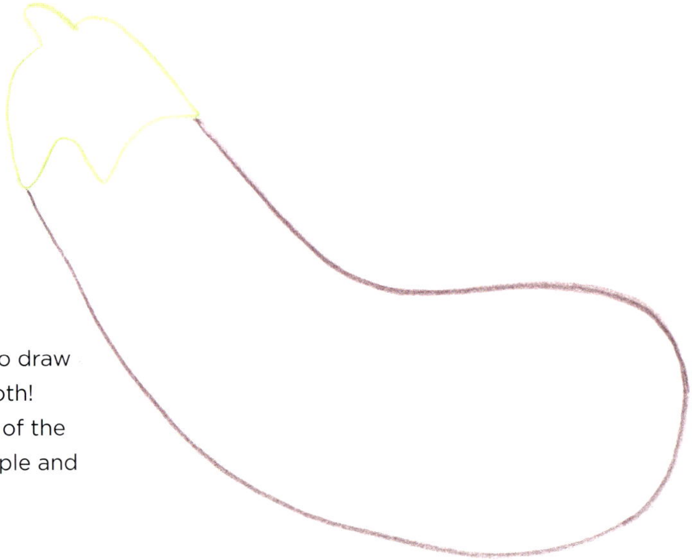

STEP 1

Eggplants are very easy to draw because they are so smooth! To start, outline the body of the eggplant with a deep purple and the stem with green.

STEP 2

The trickiest part of drawing an eggplant is getting the sheen. Lightly outline where you see the light reflecting off of an eggplant, and preserve the white. Shade in with purple around that, and fade quickly into the white sheen. Color in your stem and you're egg-cellent!

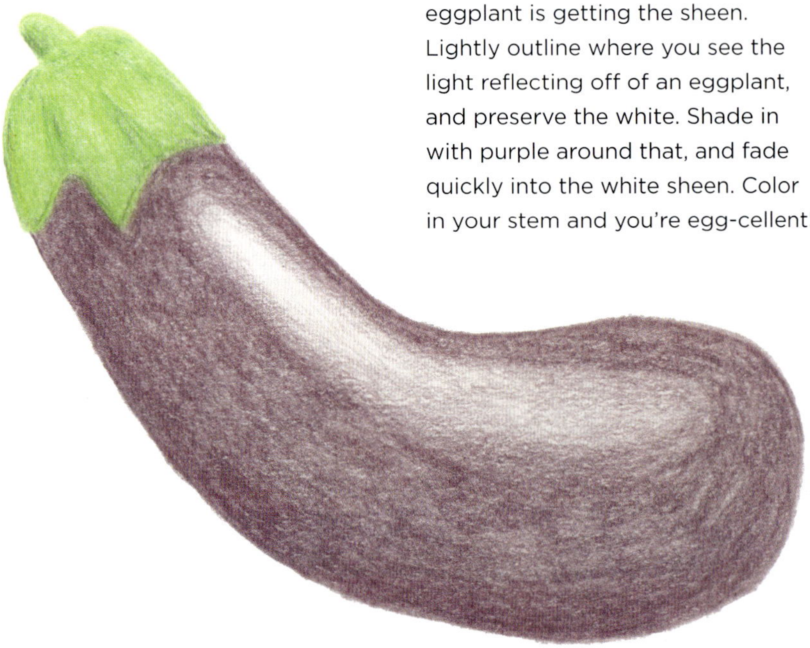

ASSORTED BERRIES

STEP 1

Contour the outline of each type of berry you would like to draw, and then study the texture and color of each.

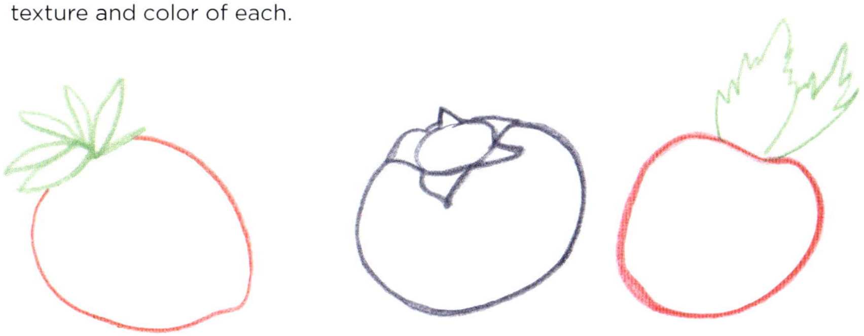

STEP 2

For a strawberry, its distinctive characteristics are the juicy red color and the seeds. You can use a black pen to make tiny seeds. For the blueberry, I noticed its grayish-blue color and waxy finish. Finally, for the raspberry, I made small circles to create its bumpy surface.

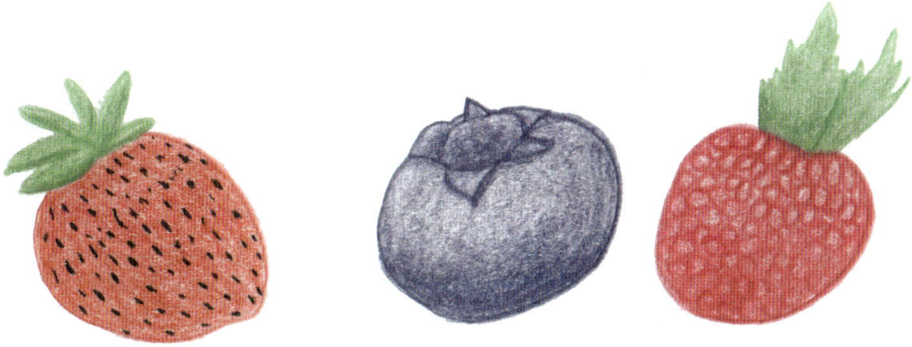

FURNITURE

Learning to draw furniture is super helpful because it can be used in so many different settings for your drawings. I love vintage furniture—especially mid-century pieces. I have a few pieces that I have learned to draw from memory and they have served me well in creating images of interesting interiors!

What makes furniture exciting to draw is its varied textures. Furniture can be made of so many different fabrics and materials.

In this chapter, you will learn to draw different kinds of fabric and create the texture of wood. These will come in handy when you branch out to draw other furniture!

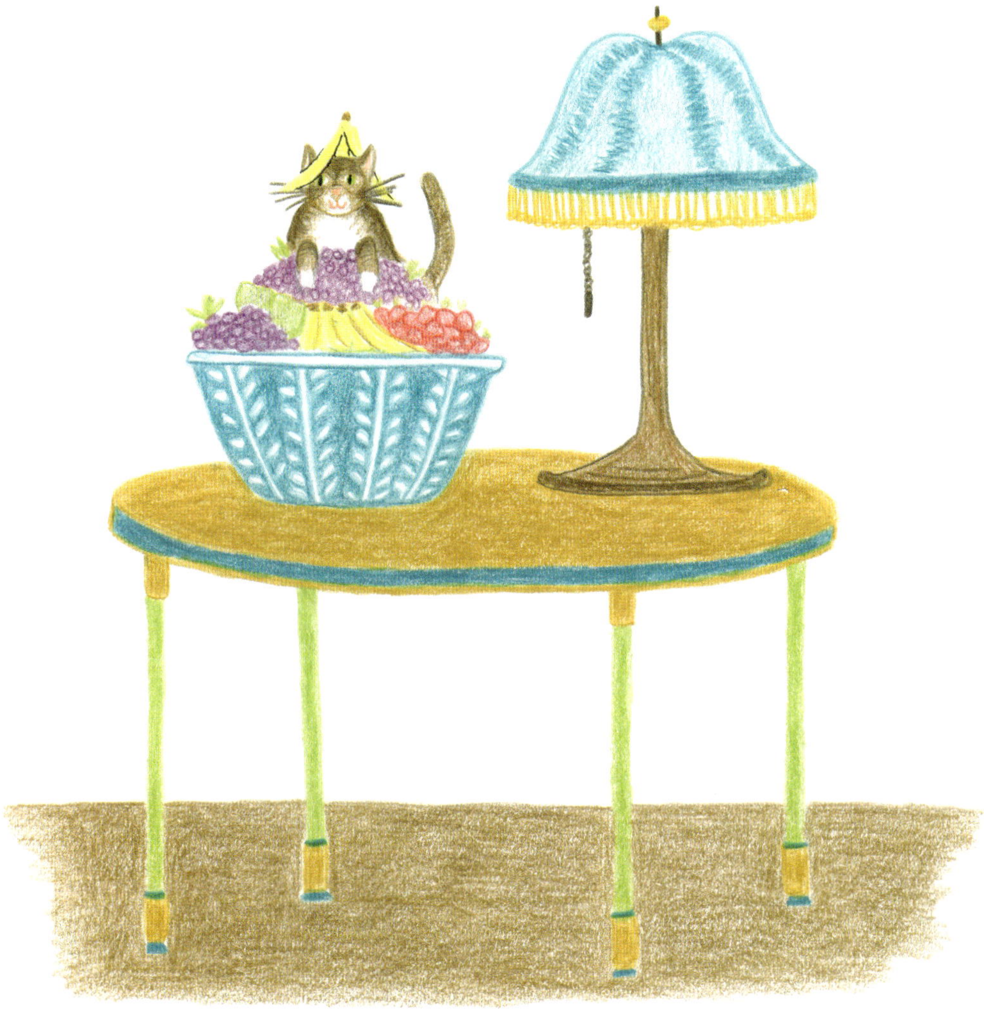

LAMP

STEP 1

I chose to draw a vintage silk lamp with many little details. To start, draw the shape of the shade. The bottom is wavy, and I drew a parallel wavy line below it to indicate where the shade's beads will end. Also, draw the basic outline of the lamp stand.

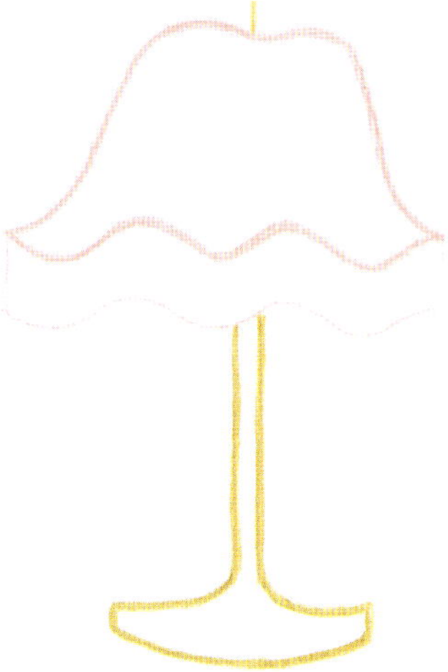

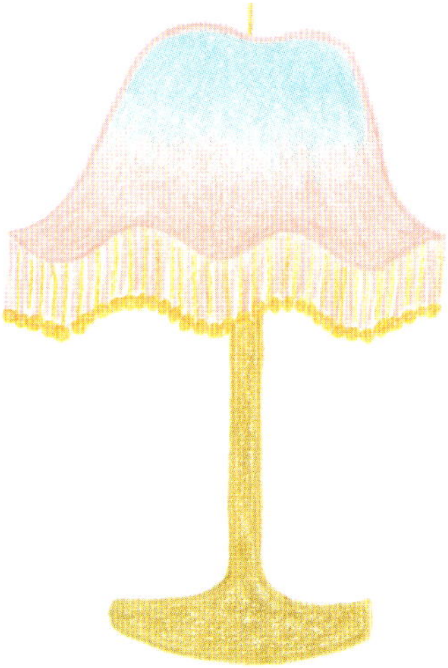

STEP 2

Next, choose a few colors that appeal to you. Shade the lampshade with two colors, and use the third color to complete the beading by making a bunch of hatch marks. Choose a neutral color for your lamp stand, and fill it in evenly.

STEP 3

Add seams to your silk lampshade, detailing on the lamp stand, and a pull chain so you can turn that light on!

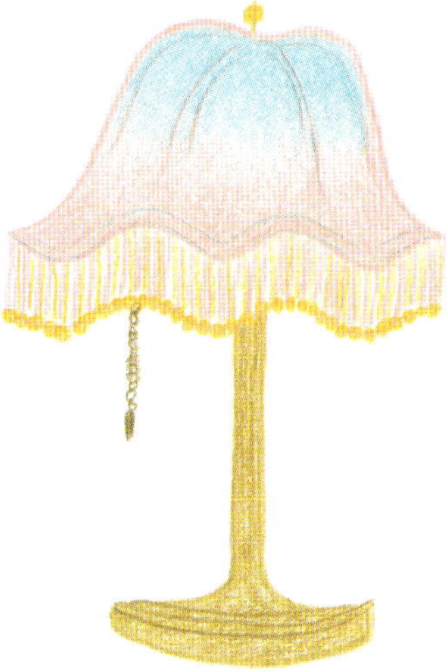

TABLE

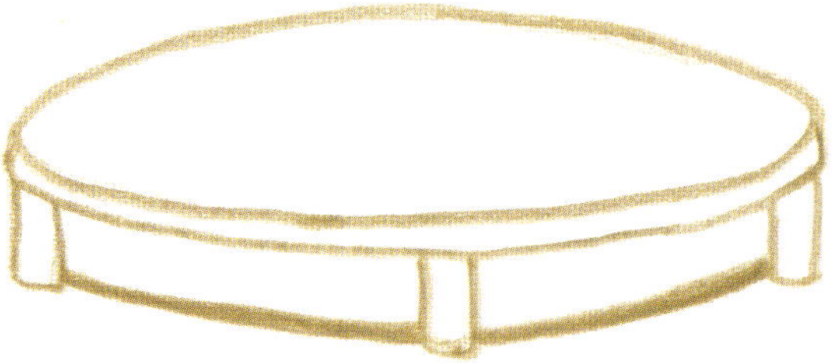

STEP 1

To start your table, use hard pressure to draw an ellipse and another line under the lower half to create dimension. Then draw three small rectangles equidistant from one another. Add another parallel curve mimicking the lower half of the ellipse.

STEP 2

Add the legs to the table. I really like long, skinny legs; I think they add a delicate touch to a table.

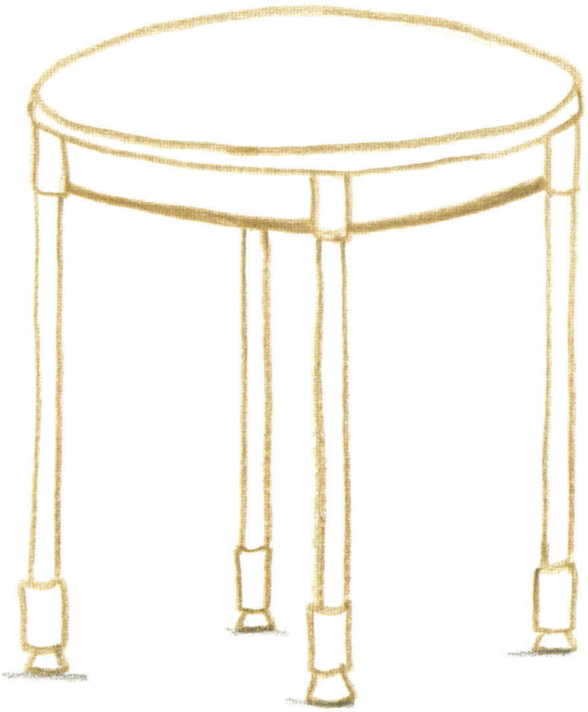

To create perspective, draw the table leg closest to the viewer the longest and the leg farthest away from the viewer highest up on the page.

STEP 3

To shade in the table with a wood-grain texture, test out the following technique on a piece of scrap paper first:

a. Use moderate pressure with a medium brown shade to create an even wash of color.

b. Then choose a darker shade of brown to put some darker lines on top, and add dark lines with the medium brown shade.

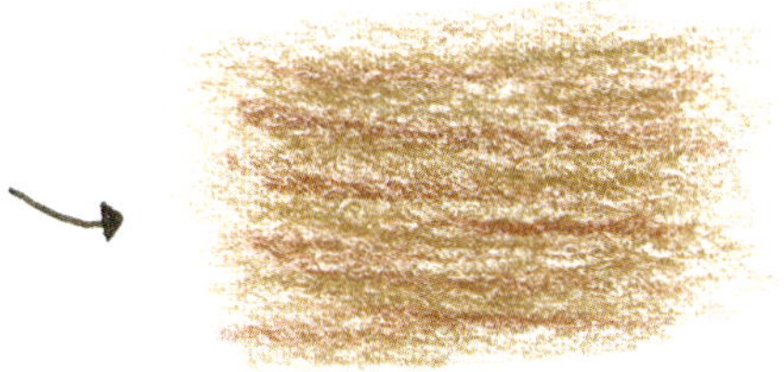

c. To blend this all in and make it look more realistic, go back over the entire swatch with the medium brown color using moderate pressure.

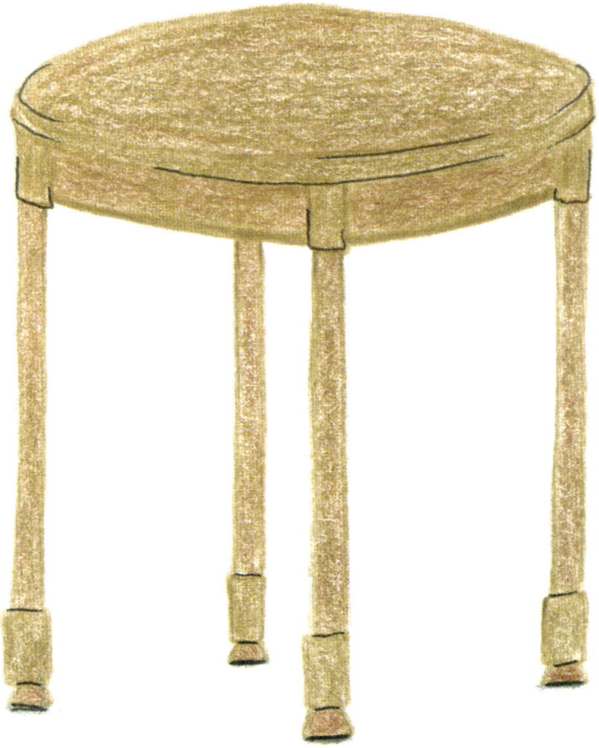

STEP 4

Fill in your contoured table with your wood-drawing technique described on page 55. I also used my pen to add details, including sharpness along the edges.

CHAIR

STEP 1

For this mid-century fabric chair with wooden legs, pick out a color for the chair that makes you happy. I love this blue color. Also, choose a brown color for the legs of the chair.

Draw the base of the fabric part of the chair by using hard pressure with your chosen color to create a boxy "U" shape with parallel lines leading off of them. See how the tops of the arms of the chair and the bottom of the right arm of the chair are all parallel to one another?

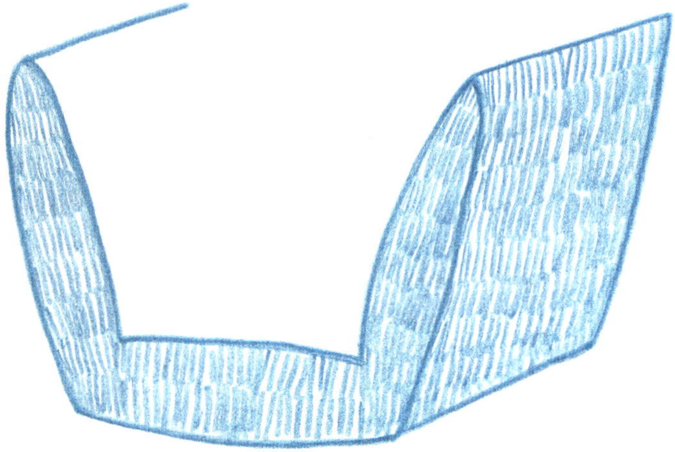

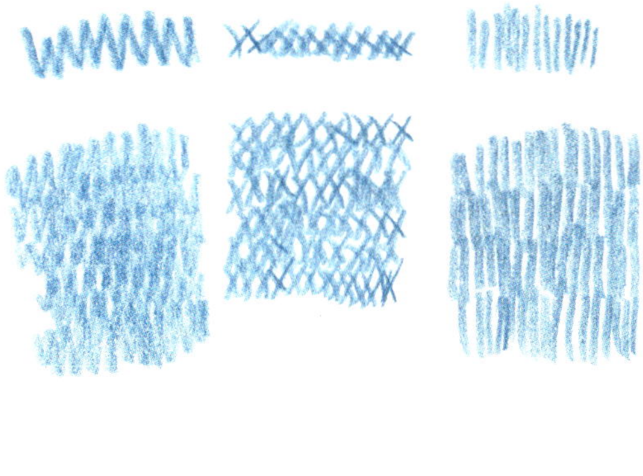

STEP 2

On a piece of scrap paper, test out some different fabric textures. I experimented with zigzag lines, crosshatching, and single-hatching. I really enjoyed the simplicity of the single-hatch markings, so I chose to fill in my chair with those.

You can apply the same techniques
when drawing any style of furniture.

STEP 3

Complete your chair by adding the back and seat cushion, and then use the brown colored pencil to contour the chair legs.

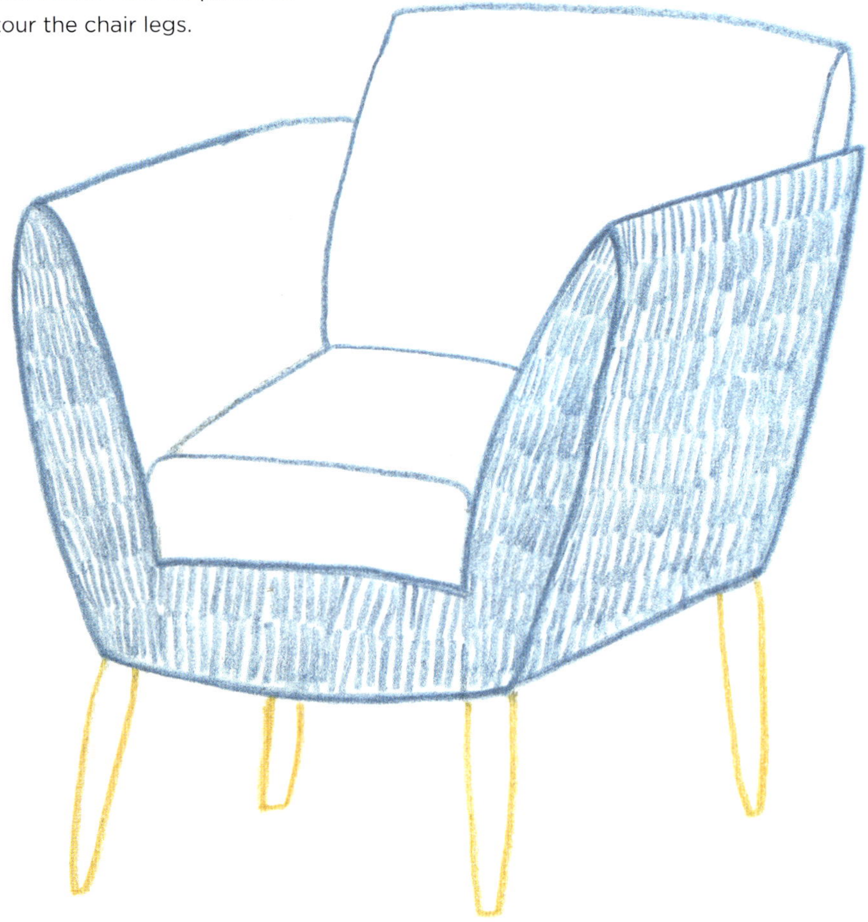

STEP 4

Fill in your chair legs with the brown colored pencil, and then complete the fabric of your chair by continuing the pattern you chose. Try to direct the flow of the pattern in the direction of the fabric. Now, kick back and relax! You've completed your comfy chair.

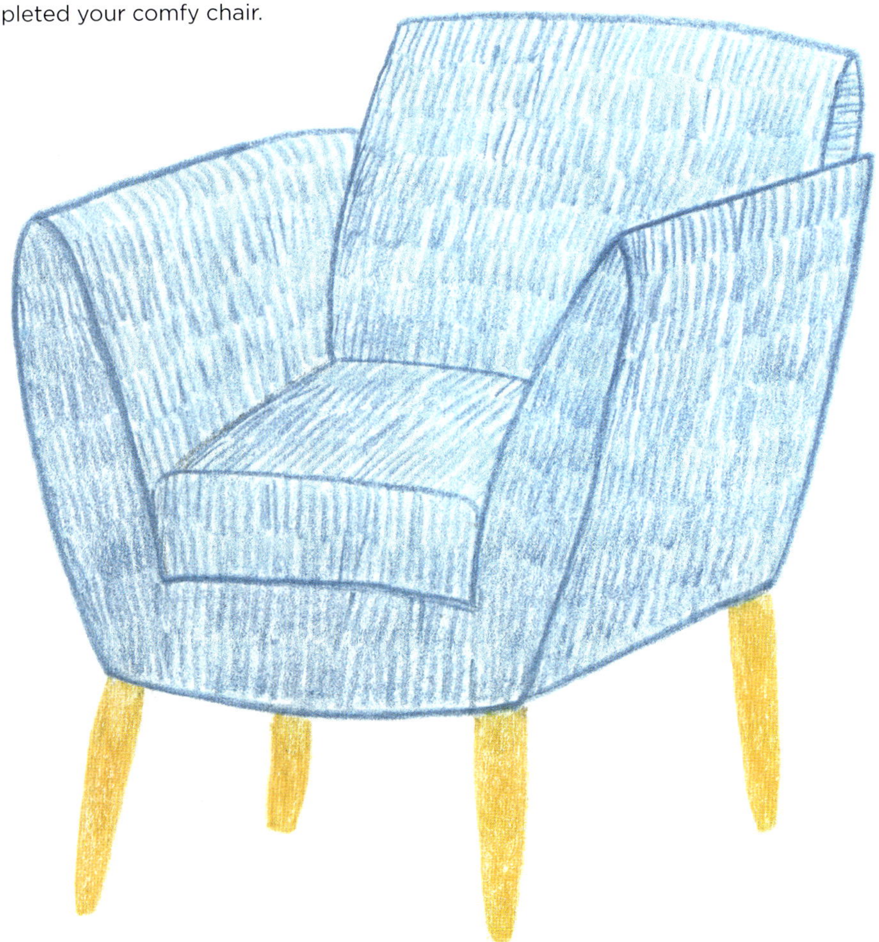

ON-THE-GO ITEMS

One of my all-time favorite things to do on the weekend is to pack up my backpack and head out on a mini adventure. This can be anywhere—my local café or park or a nearby city or village. Changing your scenery can spur an incredible surge of creativity and inspiration.

One of the great things about colored pencils is that they are so portable. I highly encourage you to pack up your pencils and draw in a new environment. Let's get to it!

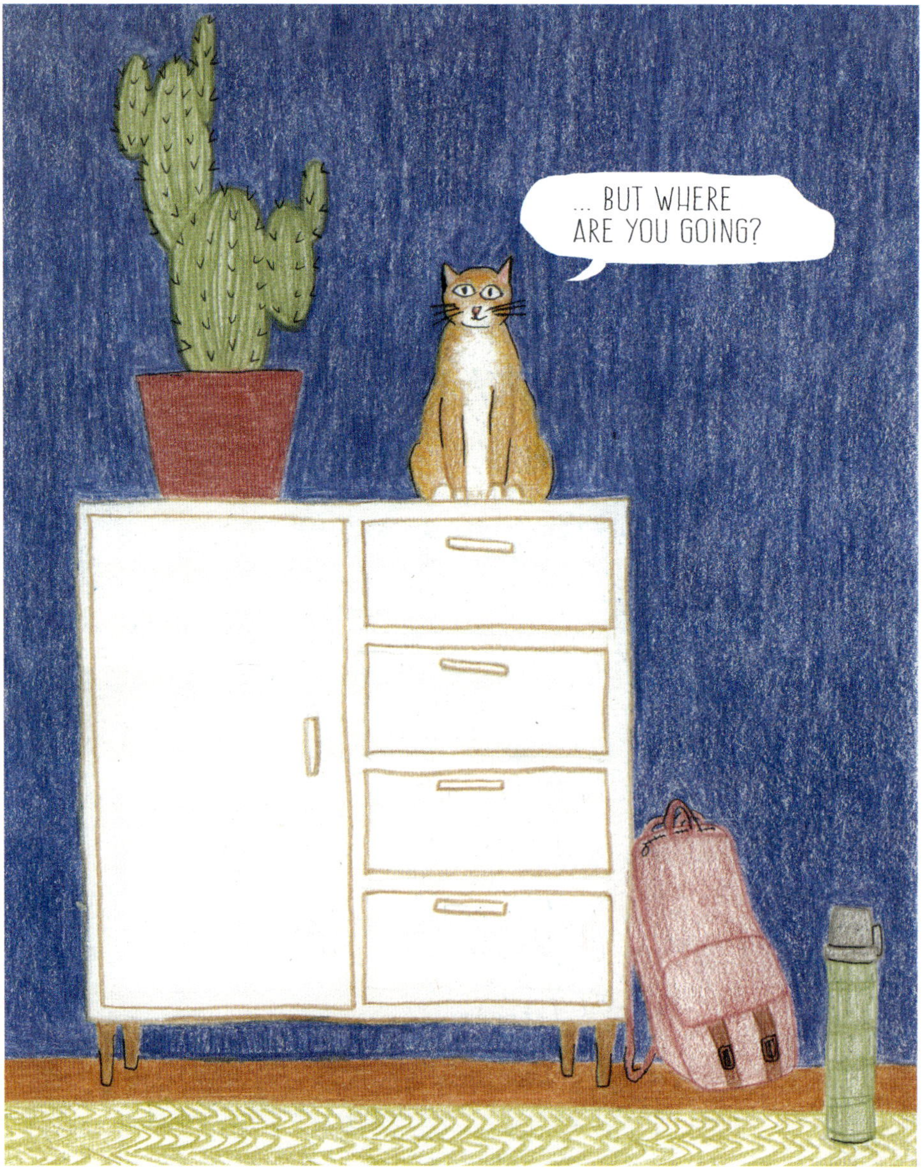

BICYCLE

What says "on-the-go" more than a bicycle? I greatly prefer the aesthetics of a vintage bicycle. I think vintage bicycles have so much character, and I love that they often come in fun, pastel colors.

STEP 1

The easiest way to draw a bicycle is to start by marking where your tires will go with a pencil. Make two circles of the same size with some space between them. By starting with the wheels, it will be much easier to keep the rest of the drawing in proportion.

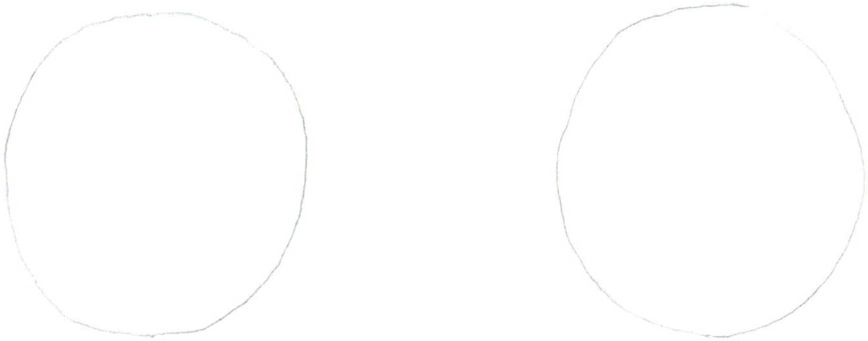

STEP 2

Choose a color for your bike frame. This is my favorite part! I chose a pastel aqua shade.

Using hard pressure, draw the wheel coverings as well as the gear cover. Notice that the back wheel covering goes over half the tire, while the front covering goes over about a quarter of the tire.

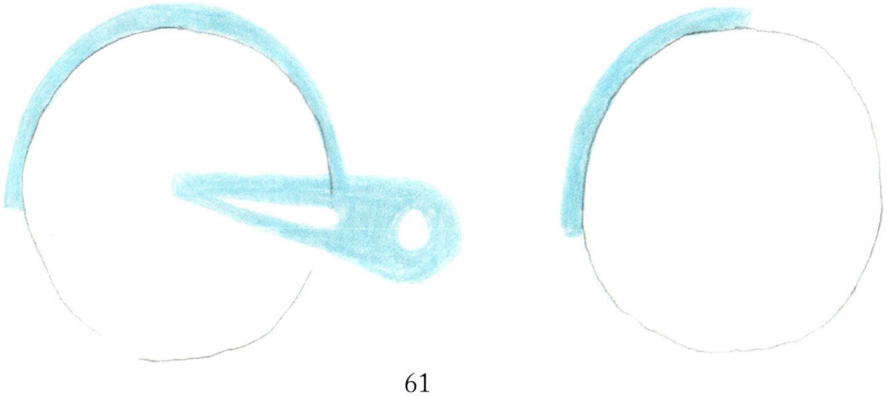

STEP 3

Next, draw two parallel slanted lines: one starting at the center of the front wheel and the other where the gear is.

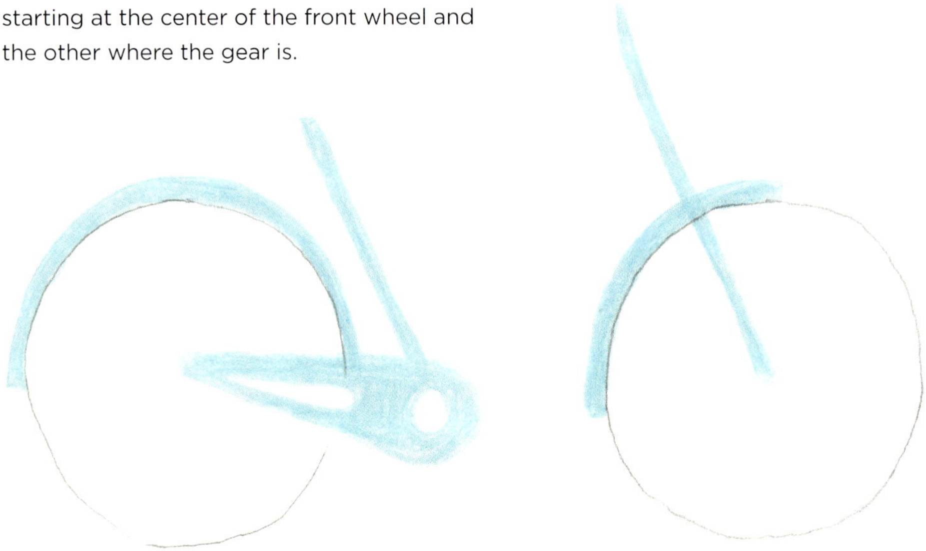

STEP 4

Add the rest of the framework, and then color in the tires with a dark gray color. Add the seat and handlebars with a neutral color of your choice. I really liked the way this orange-brown complemented the aqua color.

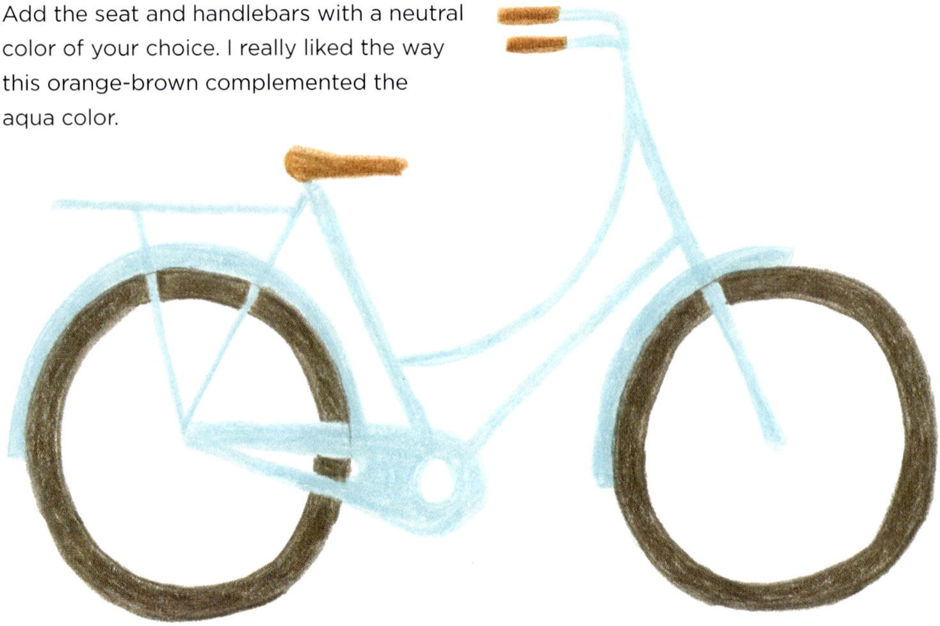

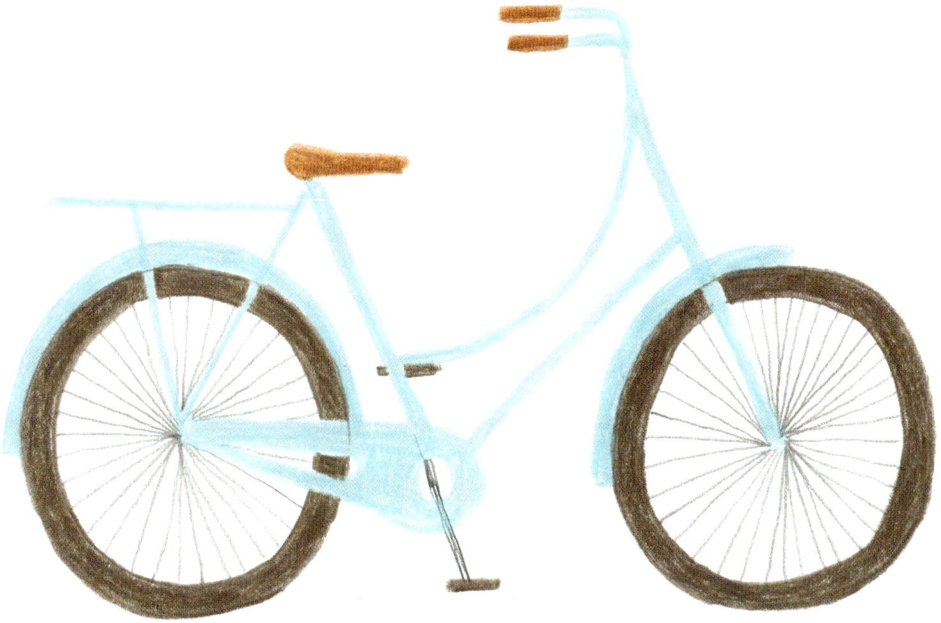

STEP 5

Finally, add your spokes radiating out from the middle of each tire, and don't forget the pedals!

Now let's pack up our art supplies so we can get out and ride that bike!

BACKPACK

STEP 1

Using hard pressure, contour the outline of the front of your backpack, including the small front pocket. Choose any color you like!

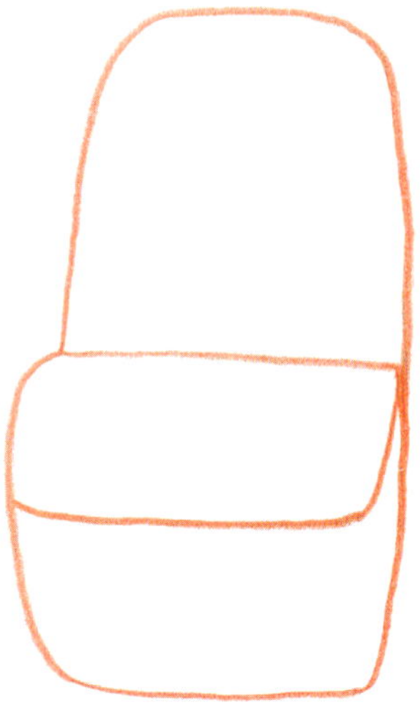

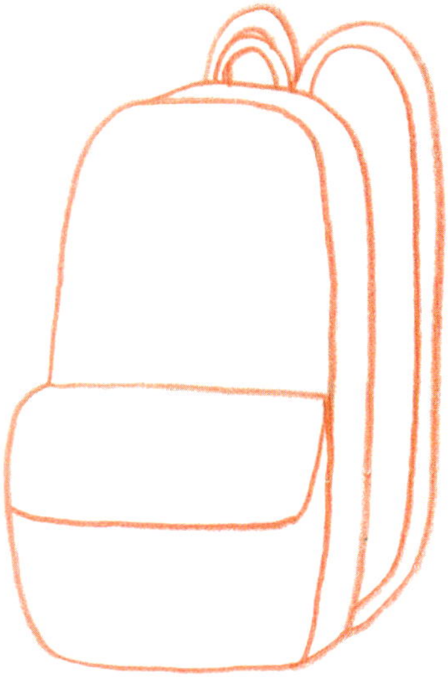

STEP 2

Next, give the backpack some dimension by adding a line to indicate its width. Then add the backpack's straps and a little hoop at the top for hanging.

STEP 3

To finish up your backpack, shade in the fabric using the back-and-forth stroking technique. Use a different colored pencil to add accent details like the buckles, zipper, and straps.

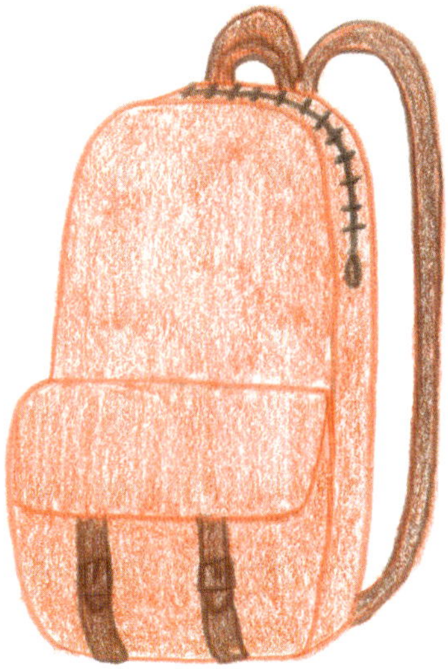

THERMOS

Thermoses may seem basic, but they offer us the opportunity to practice perspective using fill.

STEP 1

Draw the cap with a neutral colored pencil. The cap gets its depth from the contour of its lip. Fill it in with simple back-and-forth stroking.

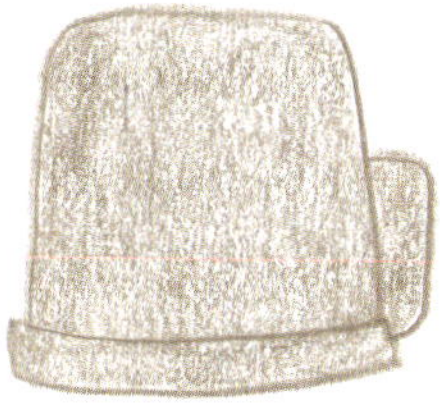

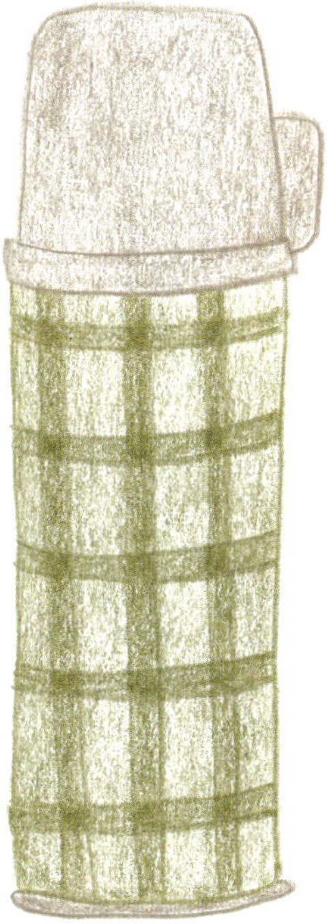

STEP 2

Then, add the cylinder of the thermos. I used a plaid pattern with slightly upturned horizontal lines to represent three-dimensionality. Notice how the curvature of the horizontal stripes in the plaid pattern matches precisely the curvature of the cap's lip.

BASKET

Picnic baskets offer us many interesting textures and materials to practice drawing.

STEP 1

Start by choosing a warm, light brown, and draw a skinny ellipse. Then draw the edge of the basket lid.

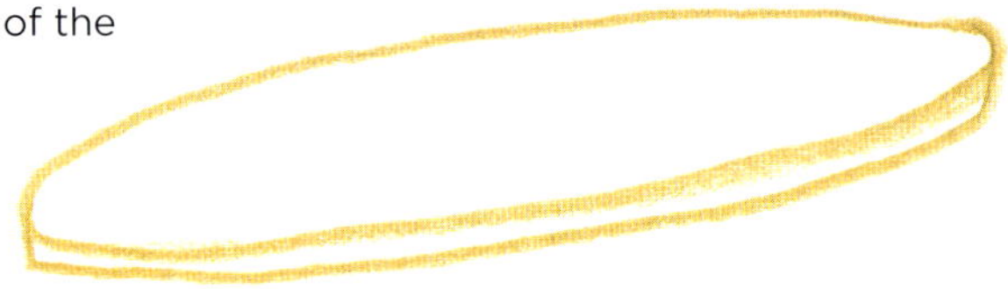

STEP 2

Draw the handle on the basket. Also, draw the cloth for your basket with any color you'd like. Next, add the actual basket outline underneath the cloth.

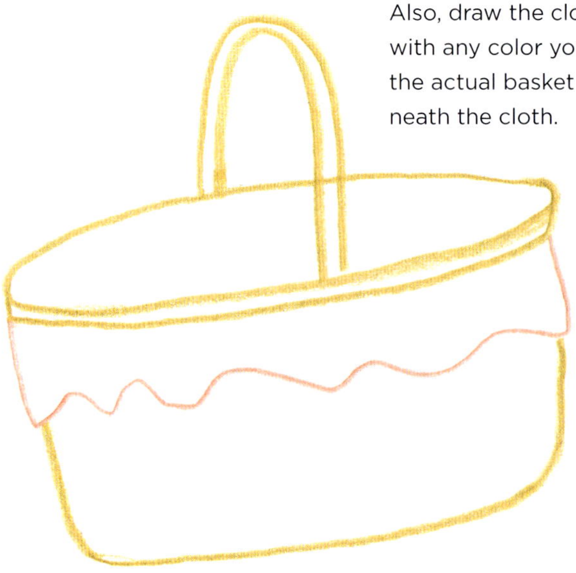

STEP 3

Draw the different fills and textures for each component of the basket. Start by filling in the lid and handle by using a standard stroking fill. Then fill in your fabric with a pattern of your choice. Finally, fill the body of the basket by hatching vertically between thicker filled lines. This gives the illusion of a weaved basket.

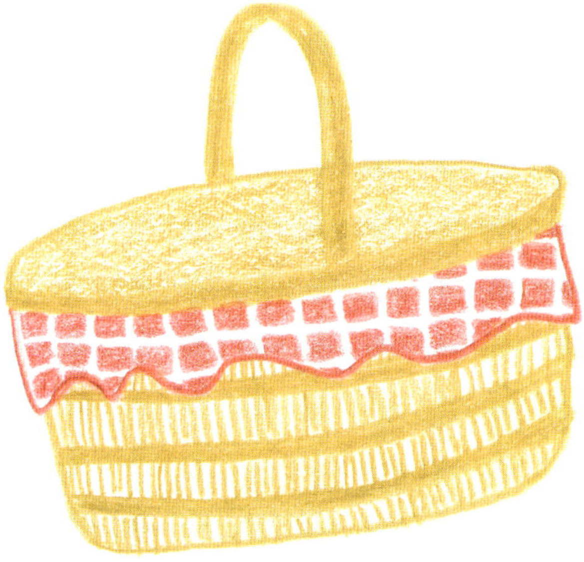

Now, what do you want to put in your picnic basket? See page 47 for an item that might be perfect for it!

PETS

Pets are fun to draw because they have so much personality and give us the opportunity to work with interesting neutral color combinations and textures. Drawing our pets helps us to connect with them. My cat, Zipper, is the light of my life and brings me so much joy. I love drawing her into my artwork. I find that adding animals to my illustrations instantly gives a piece a more personal feel.

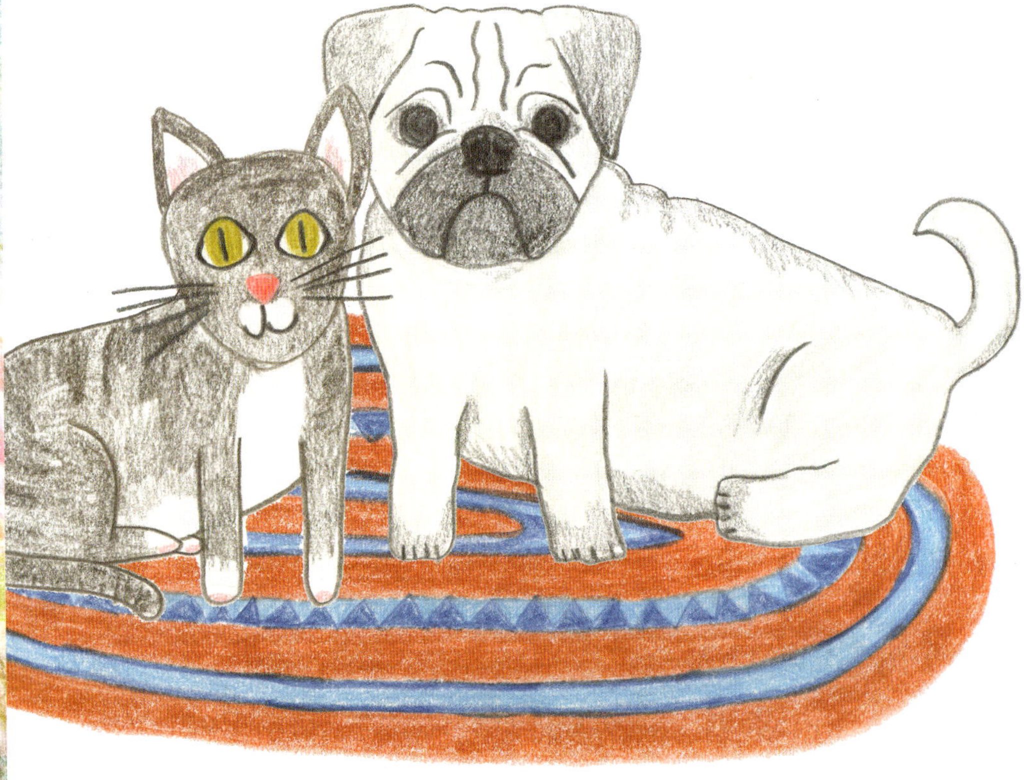

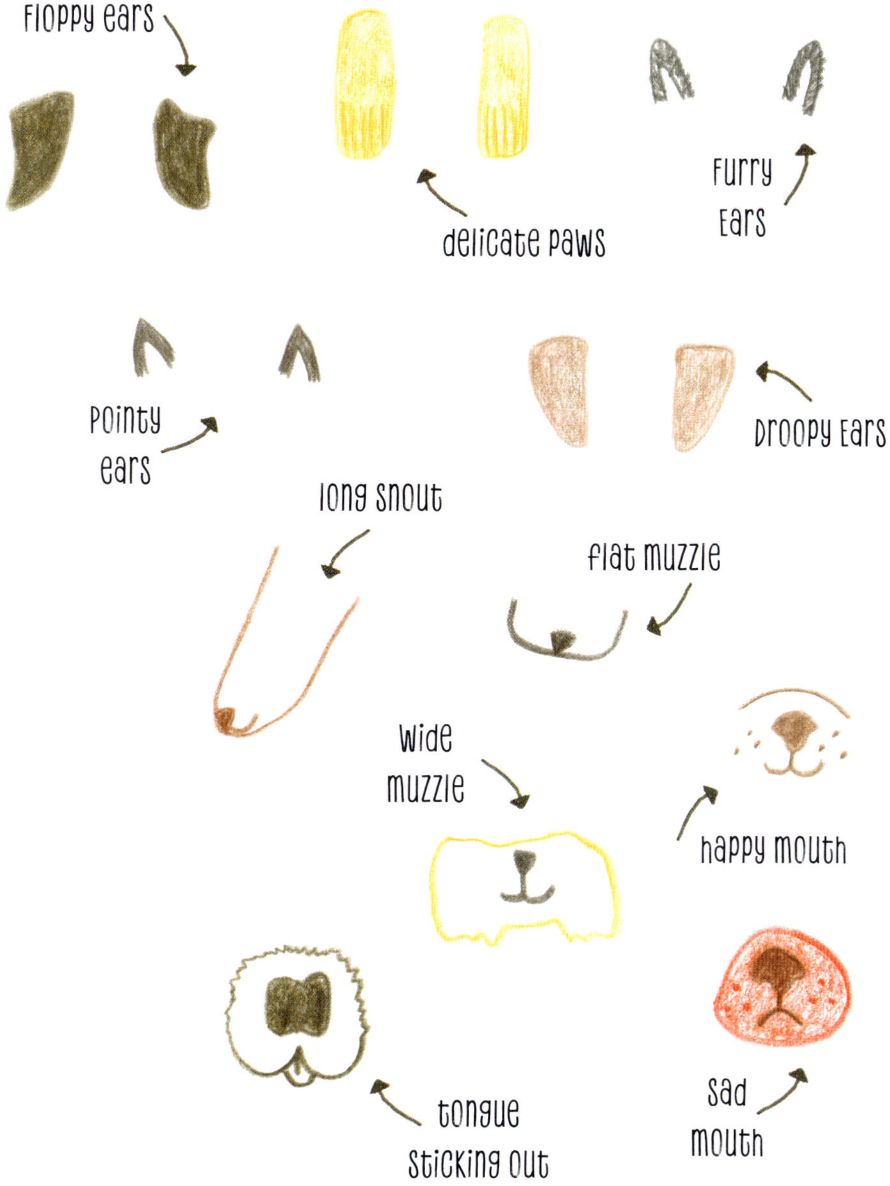

DOG DETAILS

Dogs can vary a lot in their features. The best way to practice drawing dogs is to look at different breeds and practice drawing their different features, like their ears, noses, mouths, and tails. You can go to a local dog park and sketch, or look up some online images of dogs and practice drawing at home.

CAT COMPONENTS

Cat faces tend to be structurally very similar. Their eyes are distinctively large and almond-shaped and contain a slit pupil. Their noses and mouths are much smaller in comparison.

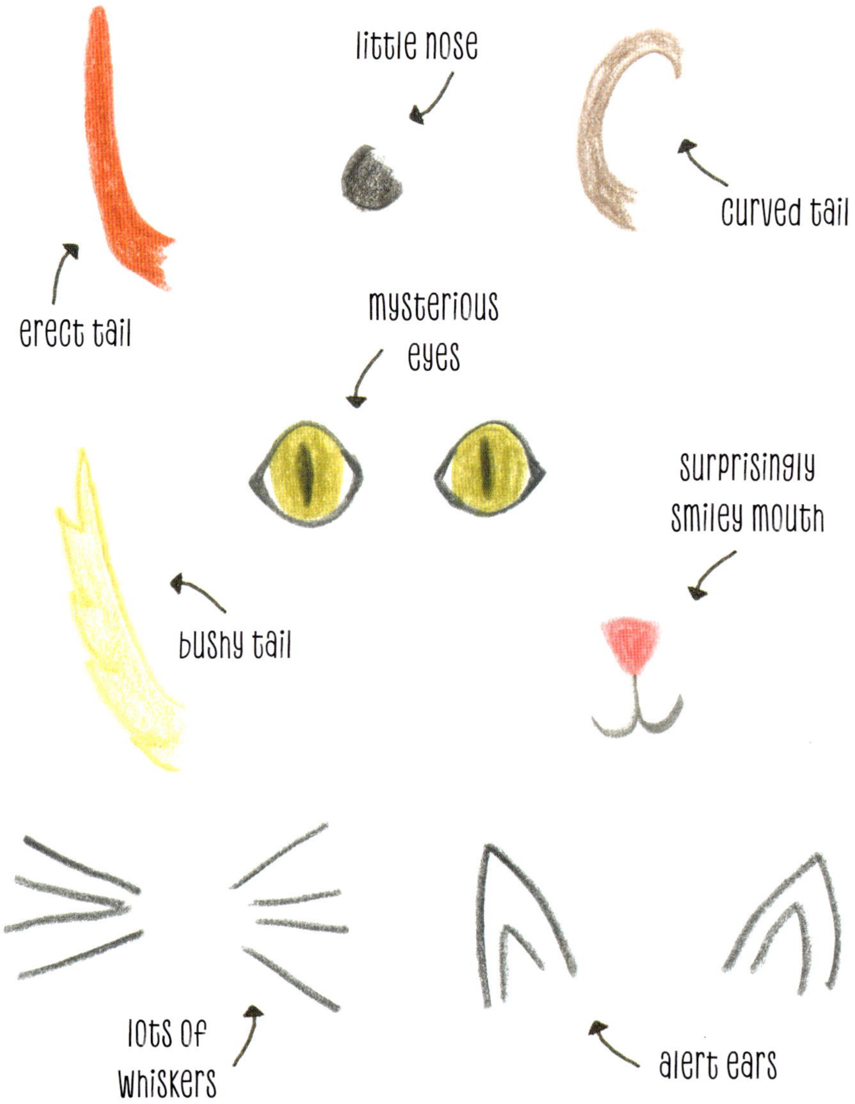

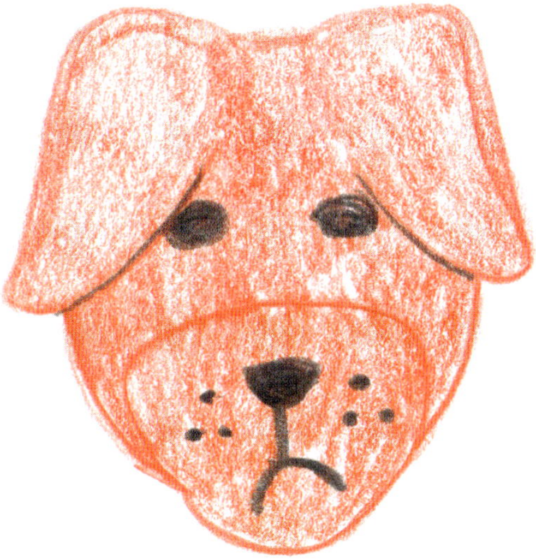

Practice drawing different cat and dog features in isolation, and then put them together to practice drawing complete faces.

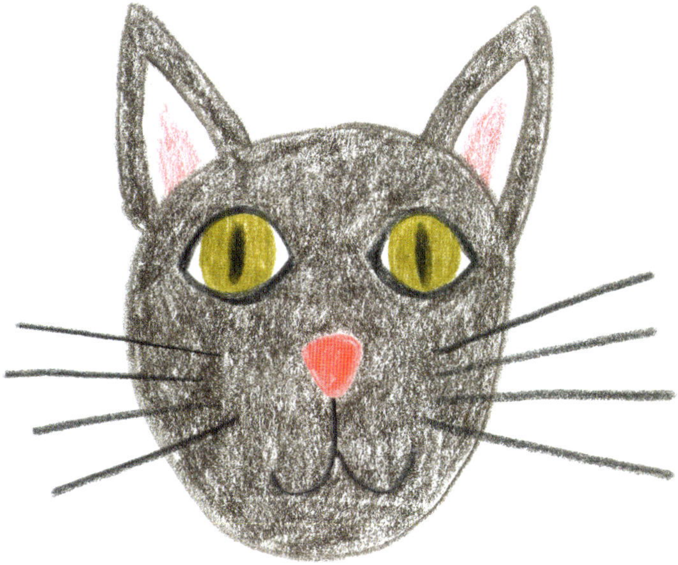

PUG

STEP 1

First, outline the shape of the body of the animal. In this example, I drew a Pug (partly because they are wrinkly and interesting to draw, and partly because they are so very adorable). Choose a blackish color for the darkest part of the Pug's fur.

To draw your animal in a seated position, draw the hind leg at an angle with a curve along the belly of the animal. When drawing the legs, note that the paw area tends to be a bit wider than the rest of the lower leg.

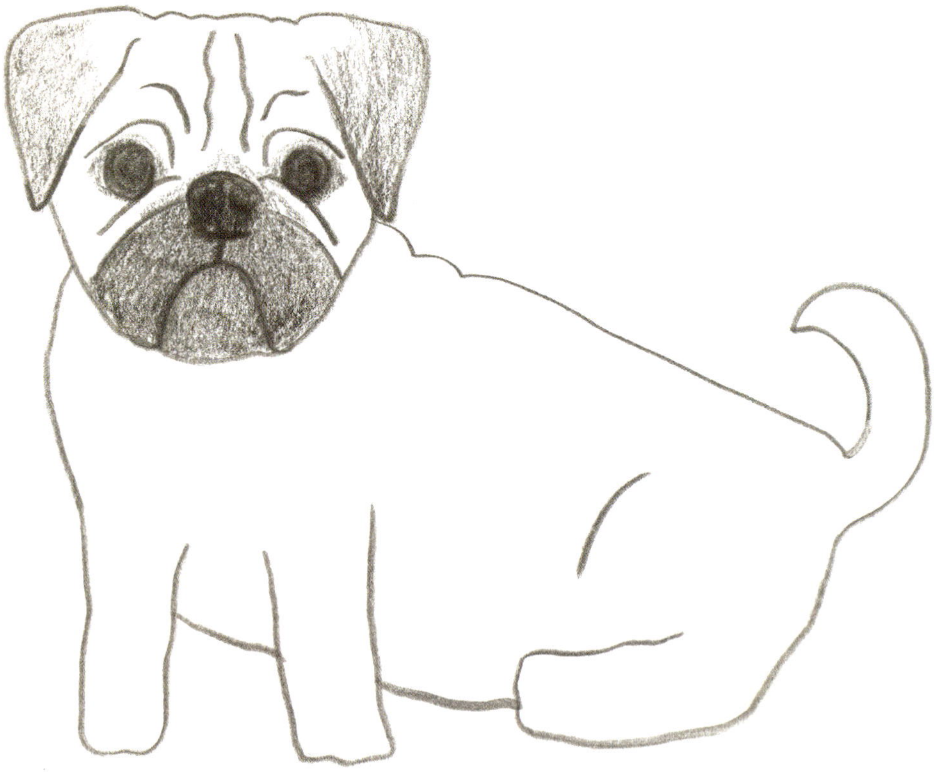

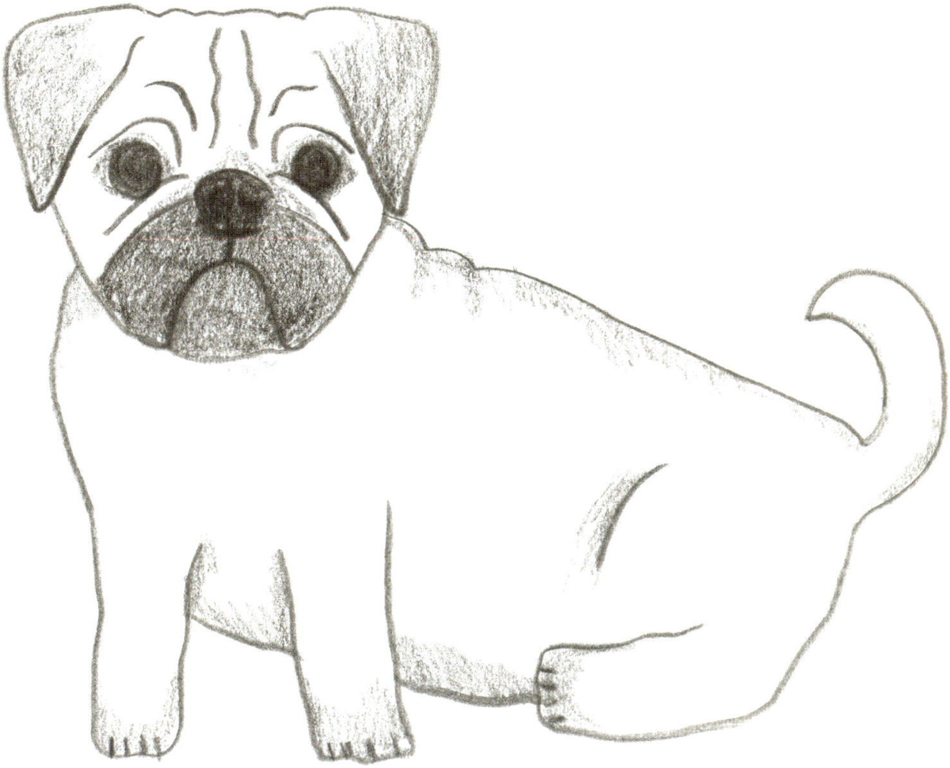

STEP 2

Next, use the same dark color to shade in areas that have darker fur. You can also add shadows on the underside of the belly and under the head, assuming the light is coming from above.

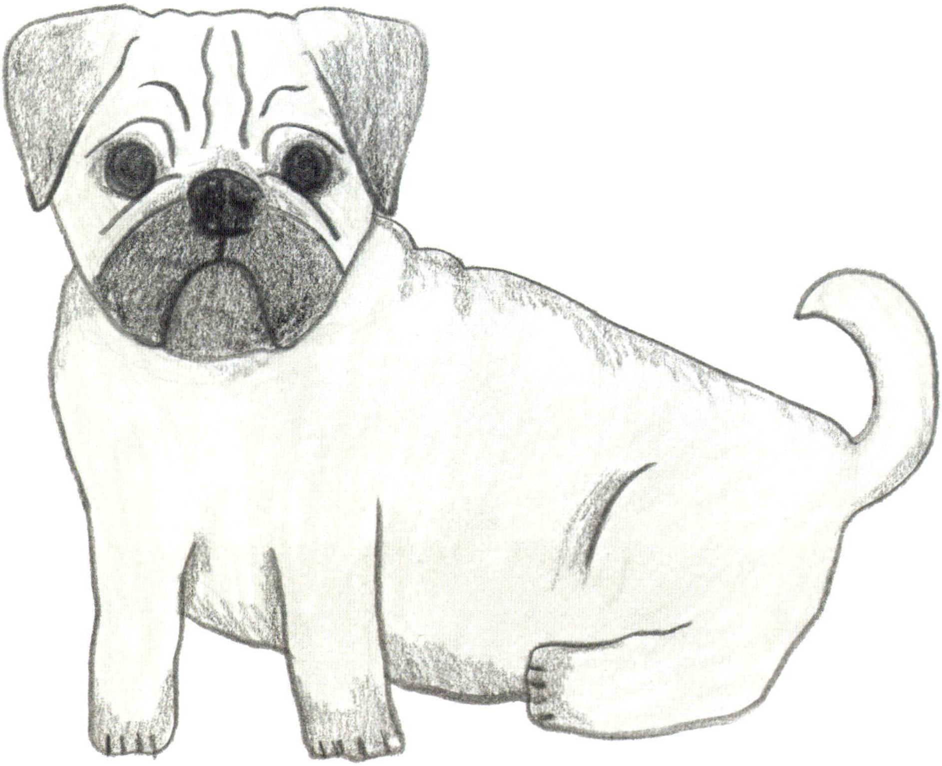

STEP 3

Finally, choose a light, neutral warm gray color to fill in the rest of the Pug's fur.

CAT FUR

Let's practice drawing different kinds of cat fur. Cats tend to differ the most in the colors and patterns of their fur, so it's important to feel confident recreating different types.

STEP 1

Draw a couple of patches of color using moderate pressure and back-and-forth stroking with a few different neutral colors. This is the base of the fur color.

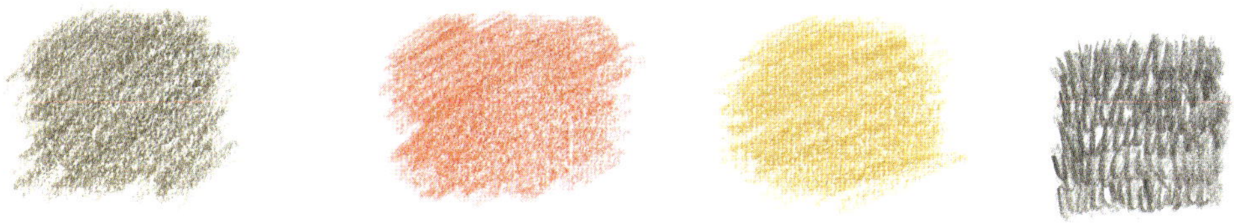

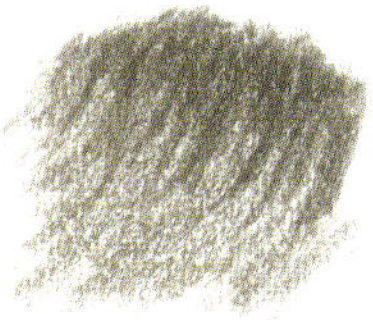

STEP 2

On one swatch, use a heavier hand with the same color and back-and-forth strokes in a slightly different angle to create stripes that stand out.

STEP 3

On another swatch, use an eraser to pull off some of the color in different spots to create an interesting spotted effect.

STEP 4

Using the same color as the base fur and a darker color, create leopardlike spots using hard pressure on a swatch. To create texture for a cat with a monotone color fur, use single hash marks.

CAT

Now let's use those newfound fur-drawing skills to compose a cat.

STEP 1

Outline the body of a cat using similar principles to those in the drawing of a dog. Use your favorite green color for the eyes and pink for the nose.

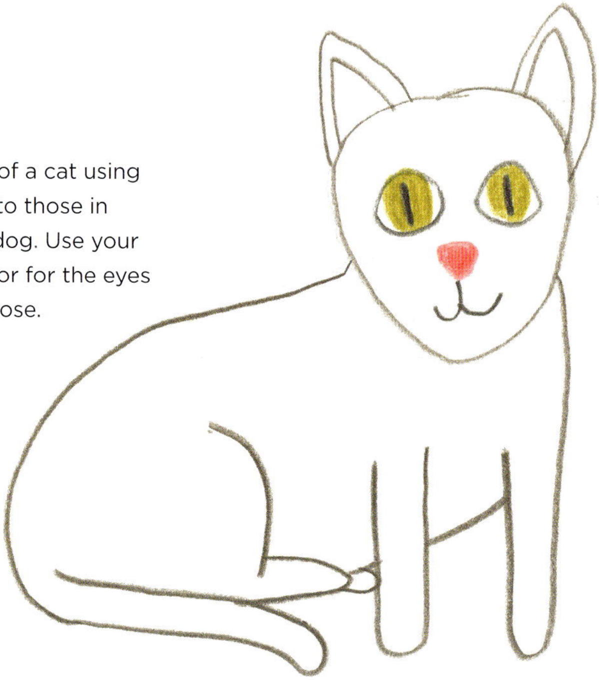

STEP 2

Practice trying different fur patterns all over!

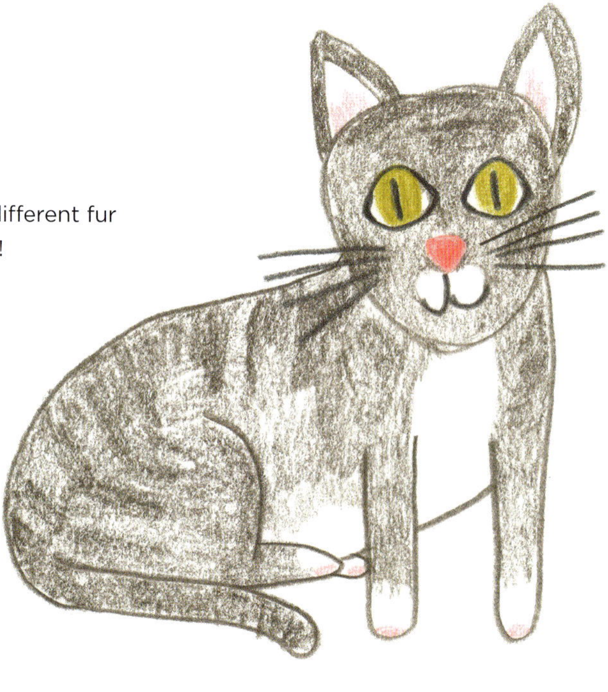

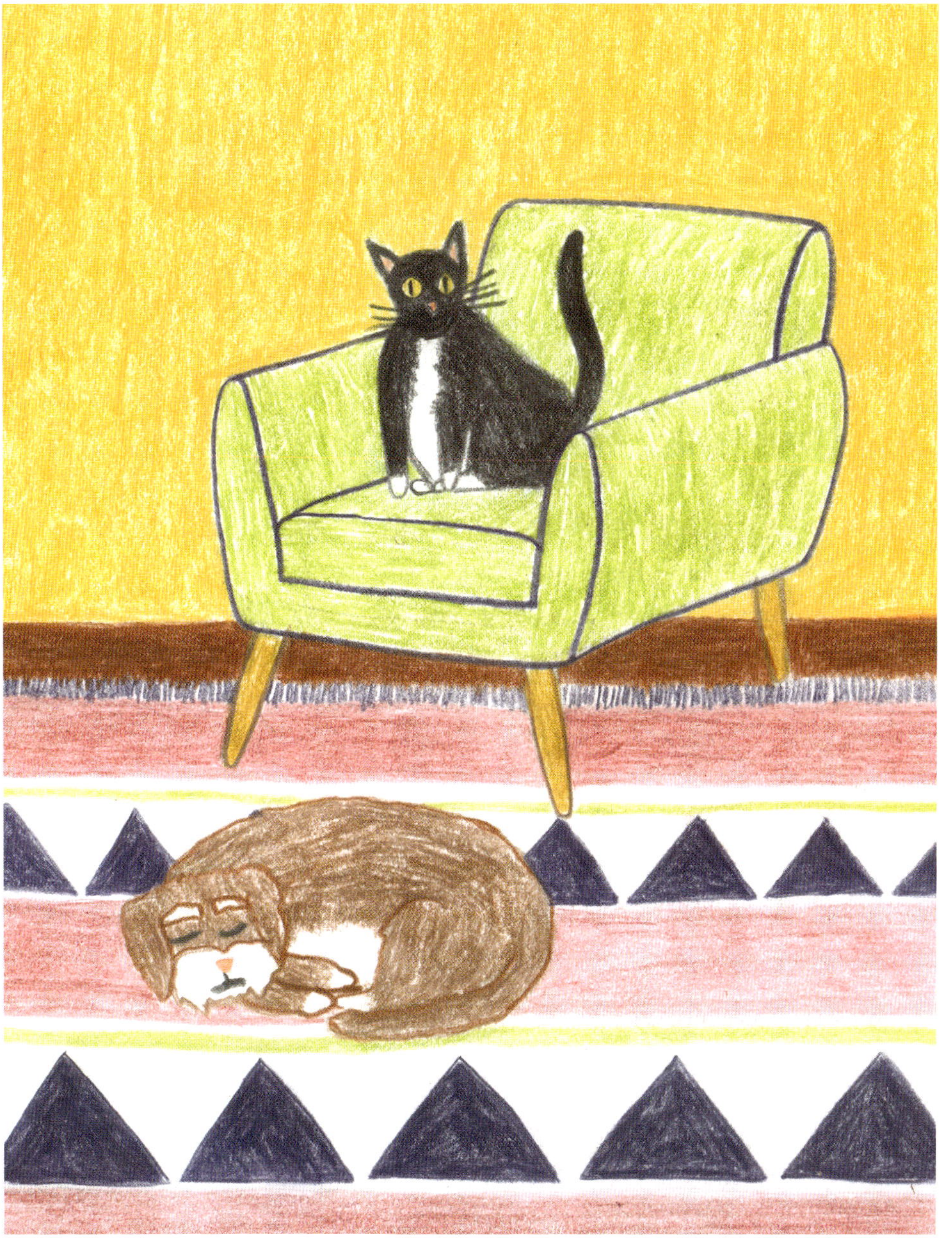

ADDING A BACKGROUND

To create a cohesive piece with a background, consider putting your pets in a living-room environment using some of the techniques and lessons learned earlier in this book. Here, I have incorporated a mid-century chair and a patterned rug. Play around with your favorite elements, and remember: There are no rules! Experiment, and have fun!

PORTRAITS

Drawing portraits was sometimes daunting to me when I was learning how to draw more realistically. There are so many elements of people's faces that make them uniquely theirs. As soon as I let go of the idea of creating a perfect, photographic portrait of a person, my portraits became more interesting and exciting.

It is easiest to examine each facial feature separately and practice before tackling a full portrait of someone. Let's take some time to look at how to draw a person's eyes, nose, and mouth separately, and then put them all together to draw a complete portrait.

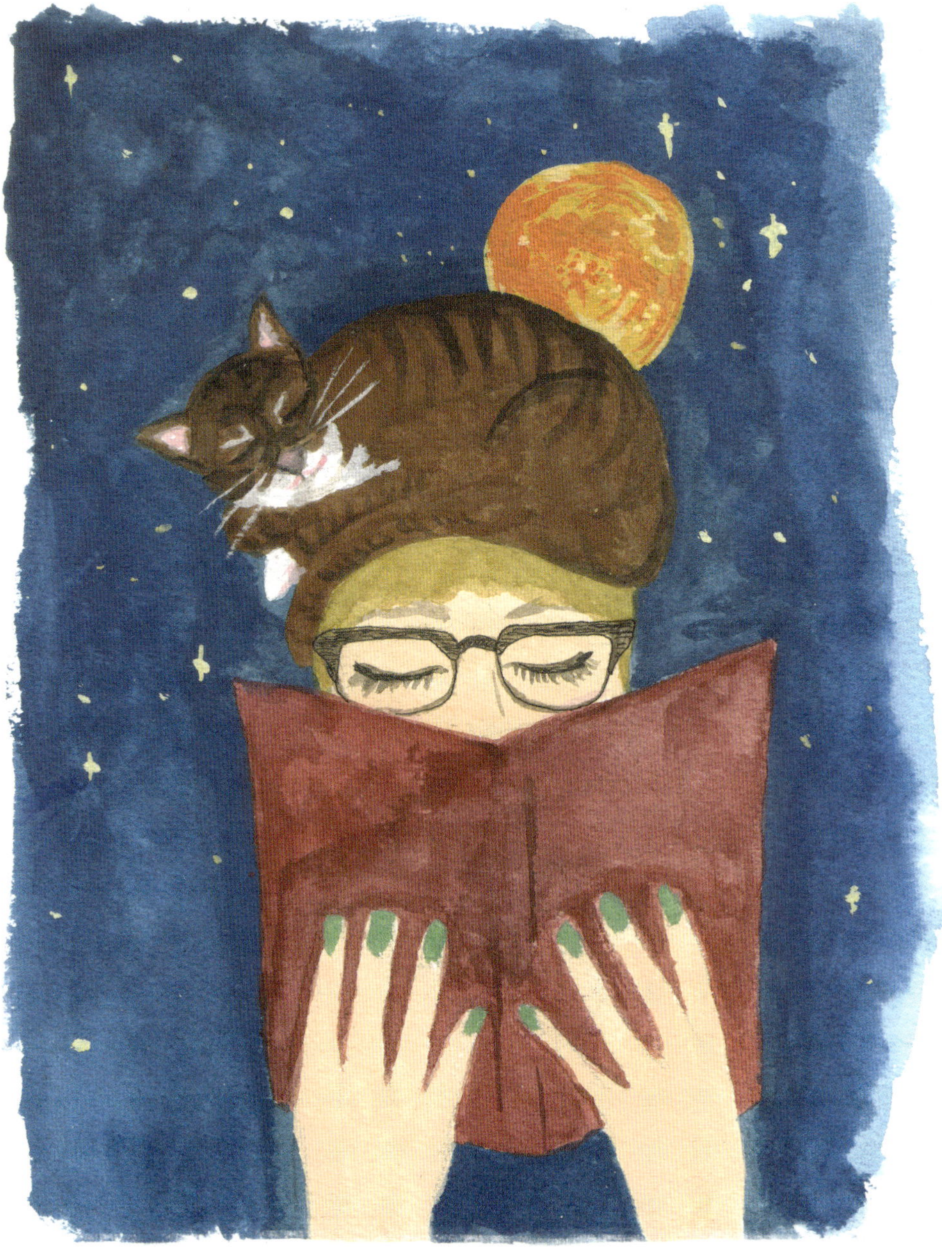

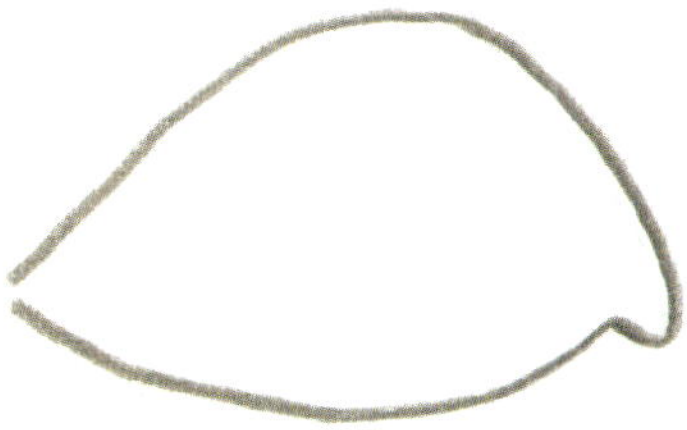

STEP 1

To draw the basic shape of an eye, I draw the top and lower edge of the eye separately. Frequently, the inner part of the upper lid is the highest part of the upper lid. Don't forget to add the tear duct.

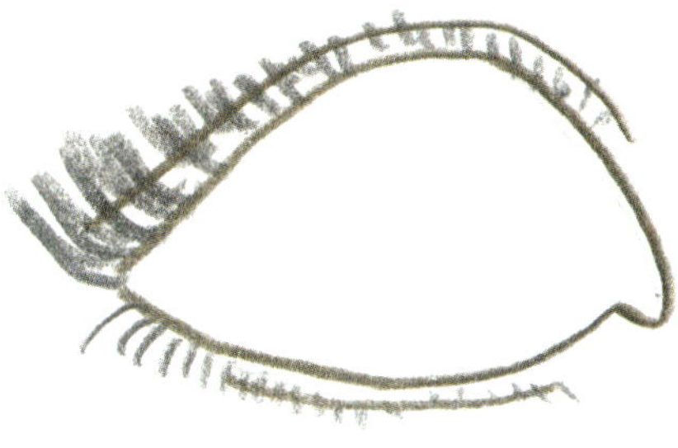

STEP 2

Next, add a line above the upper edge of the eye to create the upper eyelid and a short line below the lower line to indicate the lower lid. Then add your lashes with a dark brown or black colored pencil. The lashes toward the outer edge are the longest!

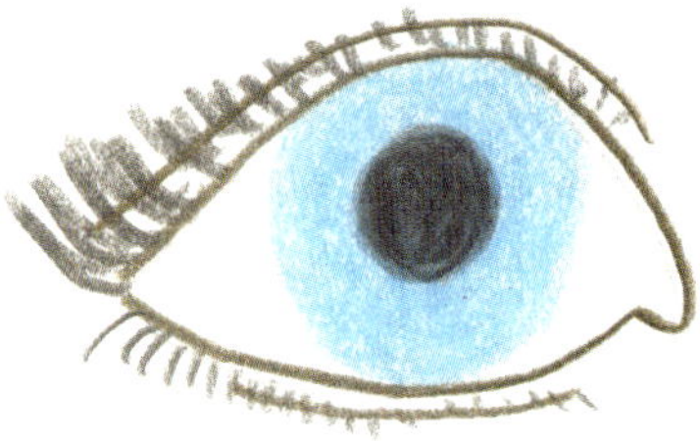

STEP 3

Draw the round iris, and fill it in with your favorite eye color. The iris should be partially obscured by the eyelids. With a black colored pencil, add a pupil to the eye. Finally, add some shading in darker areas, including on the upper lid, near the tear duct, and the bridge of the nose.

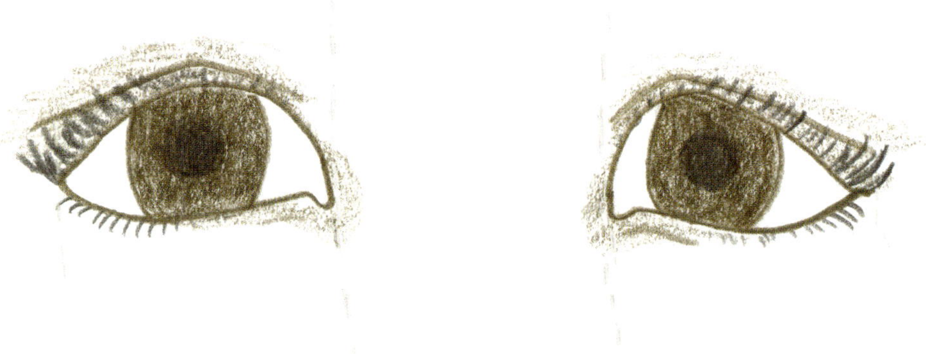

When drawing the eyes in a portrait, draw them approximately one eye's width apart.

NOSE

The biggest issue people have with drawing noses tends to be that they draw too much detail. When drawing a nose from the front, the bridge shouldn't be strongly indicated. Focus on drawing the bottom of the nose and the nostrils. Here are a few examples of different nose shapes. In profile view, you are able to see distinct differences in the bridges of the noses.

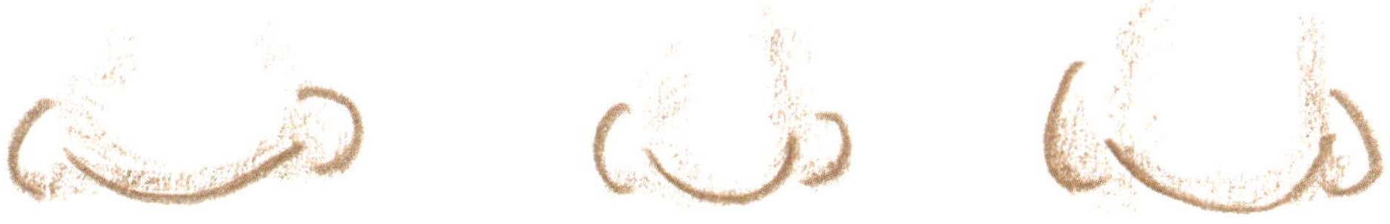

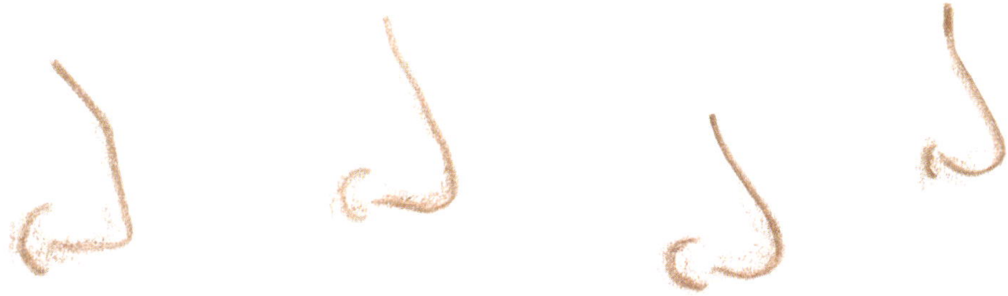

MOUTH

Similar to drawing noses, when drawing mouths, less is more. If you draw the entire outline of the lips, they tend to look detached from the rest of the face. Draw the line of the upper edge of the upper lip, especially around the cupid's bow, and a line where the two lips meet. Then draw a very short line with soft pressure to indicate part of the bottom of the bottom lip. Shade in the lips from the center, and lighten the pressure as you move toward the outer edges of the lips.

PROPORTIONS OF THE FACE

A few guidelines are important to follow when drawing various features onto a face. These include:

1. The eyes are halfway down the head and one eye's width apart from one another.
2. The bottom of the nose is halfway between the eyes and the bottom of the chin.
3. The mouth sits just above the halfway mark between the bottom of the nose and the bottom of the chin.
4. Ears, if shown in your portrait and depending on hairstyle, should be drawn starting in line with the eyes and ending near the bottom of the nose or mouth area.

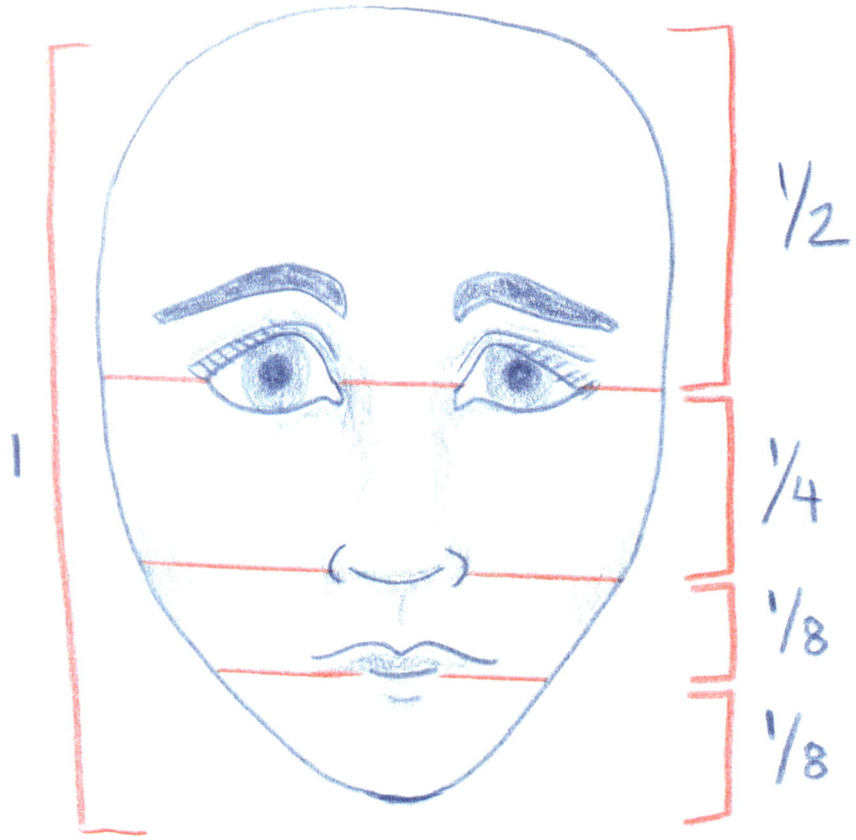

PROPORTIONS OF THE BUST

When drawing the rest of the bust of your portrait, note that the neck is almost but not quite as wide as the head. Also, women's and men's shoulders tend to be differently shaped. In general, men's shoulders are broader, although no two people are alike.

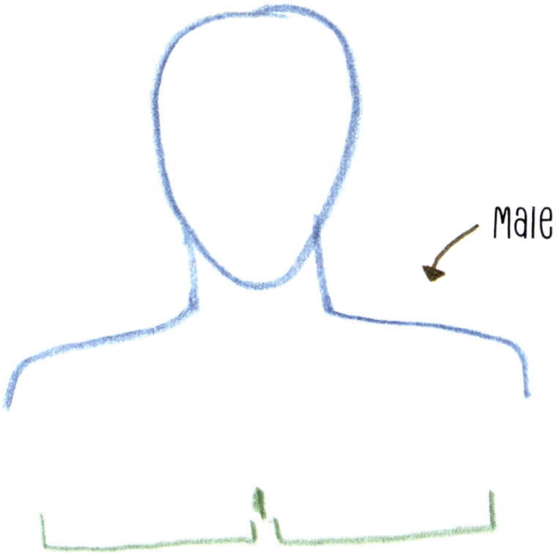

It's best to draw from life or photographs and use these tips as guidelines.

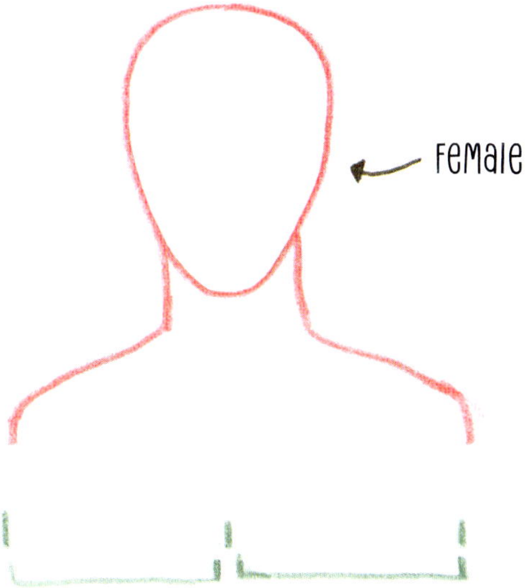

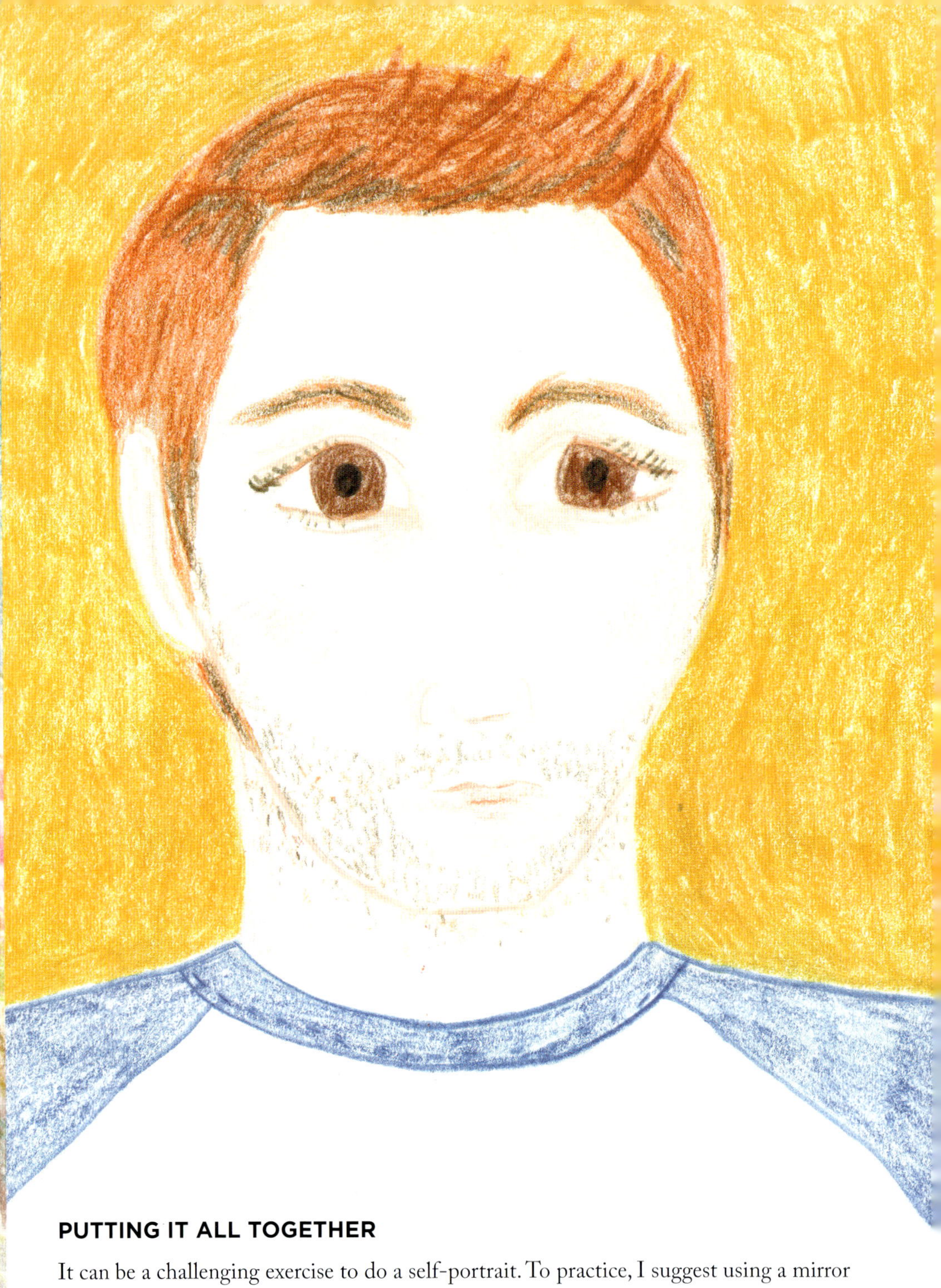

PUTTING IT ALL TOGETHER

It can be a challenging exercise to do a self-portrait. To practice, I suggest using a mirror instead of a photo of yourself. Test out some of these techniques, and see how you are able to represent yourself. If a friend or family member has some time, offer to draw him or her! The more you can practice drawing different people, the more you'll get a feel for catching the energetic essence of a person.

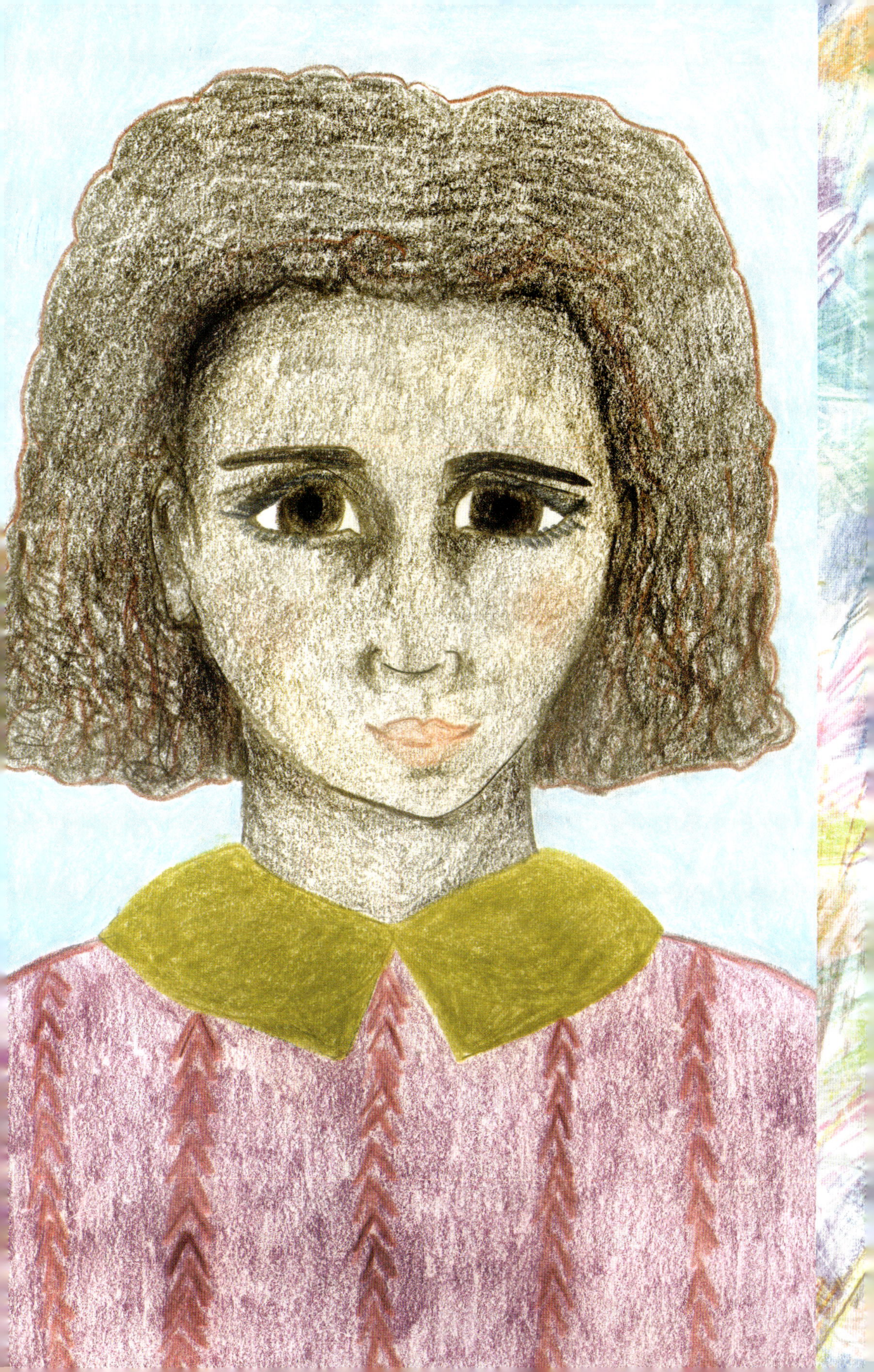

CAMPERS

I've never been a huge fan of camping, but I do have a deep appreciation for nature and the great outdoors. I love looking at photographs of other people's camping excursions, and I'm particularly enamored with vintage campers. They're so quirky and kitsch, which makes them great subjects for illustration!

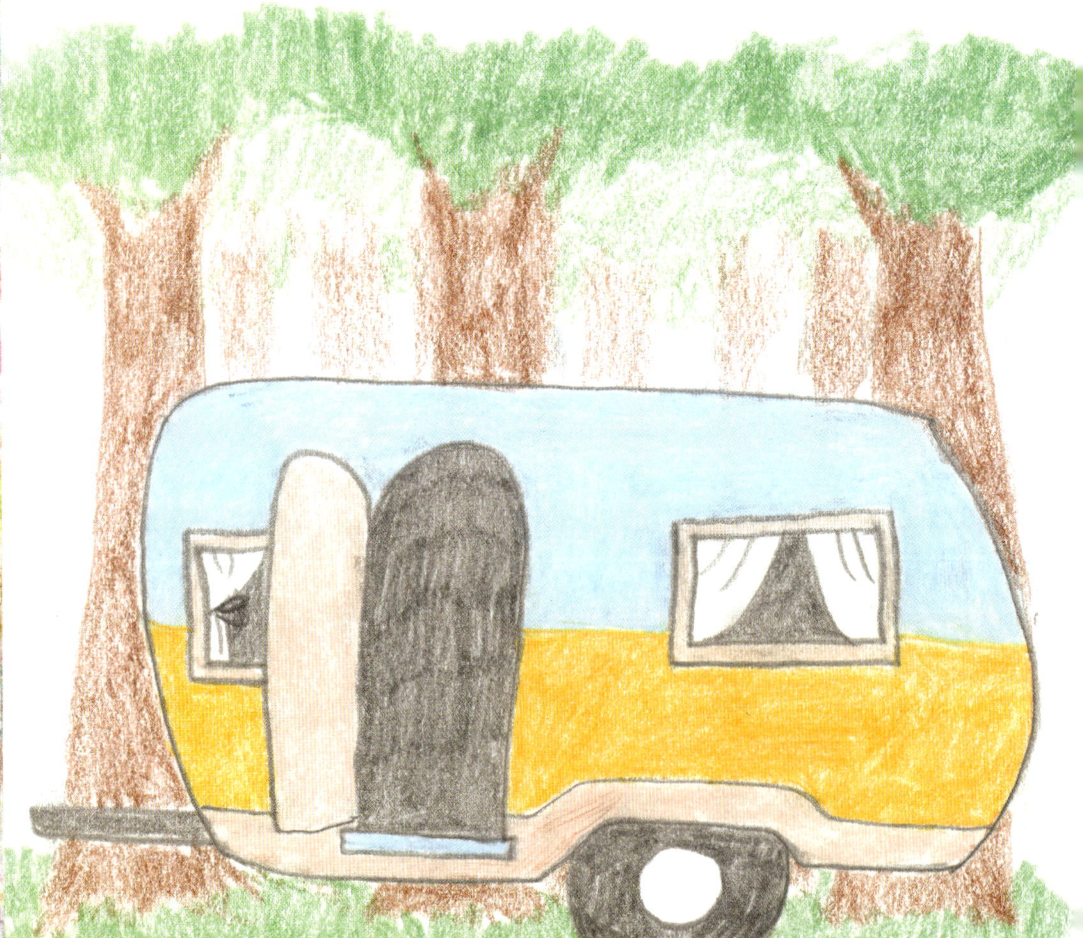

COLOR CUES

Many vintage campers look aesthetically pleasing because of their rounded shape and soft, pastel colors. Before starting to draw a camper for this exercise, pull a handful of pastel colors from your colored pencil set, and experiment with different combinations of these.

Pastels are easy to work with because their pale colors make them very easy to combine into a color palette.

TRAILER

STEP 1

Use a graphite pencil or a metallic or gray shade of colored pencil to draw the outline of the camper's body and wheel. This gray shade will indicate the metal from which the camper is manufactured.

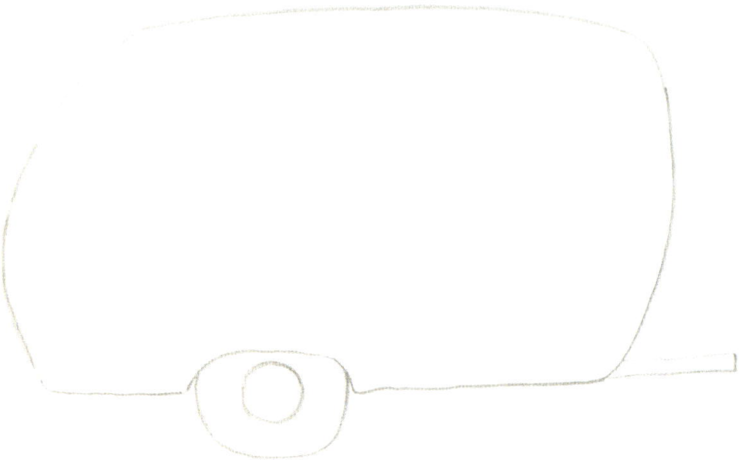

STEP 2

Next, use the same pencil to add some details for the camper, such as the windows, a door, and curtains in the windows.

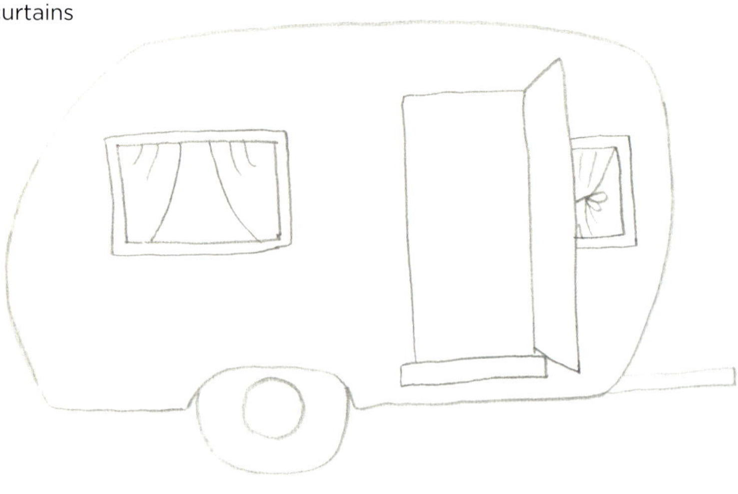

STEP 3

Adding a line along the inside of the camper's body implies metal detail accents. Color in your camper's wheel while you're at it!

Then fill in the space between the curtains and the open door with your pencil to create the illusion of depth.

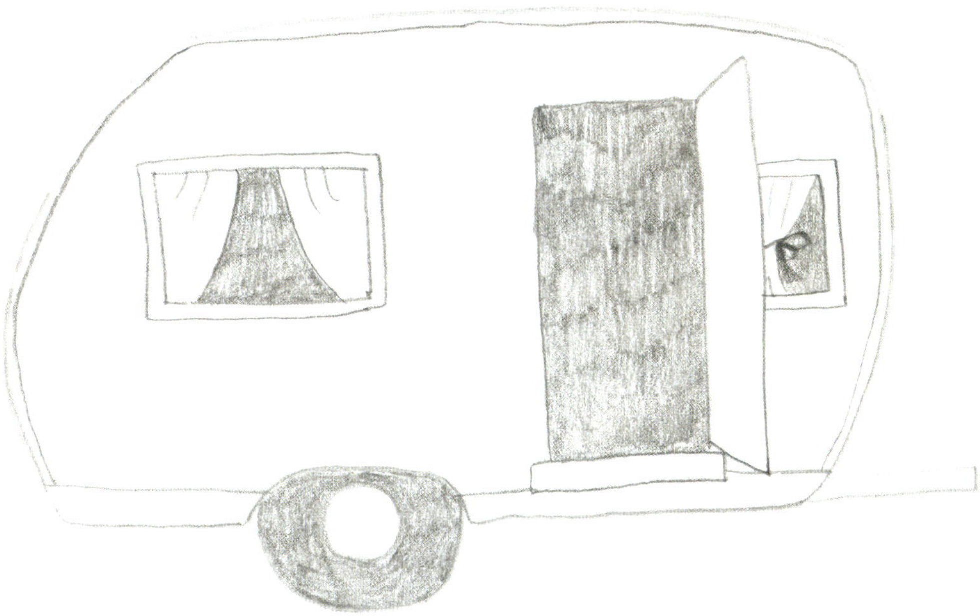

Adding an open door creates a warm, welcoming feel in your drawing.

STEP 4

Choose a favorite color combination from your pastel experimentations on page 87, and add bars of color to your camper to create a minimalist color palette and retro feel!

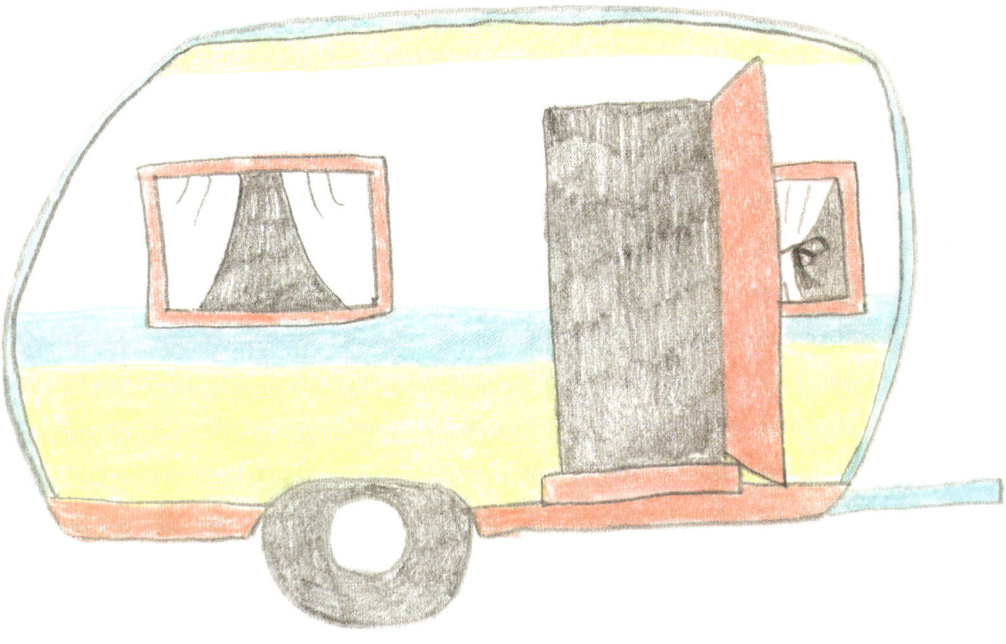

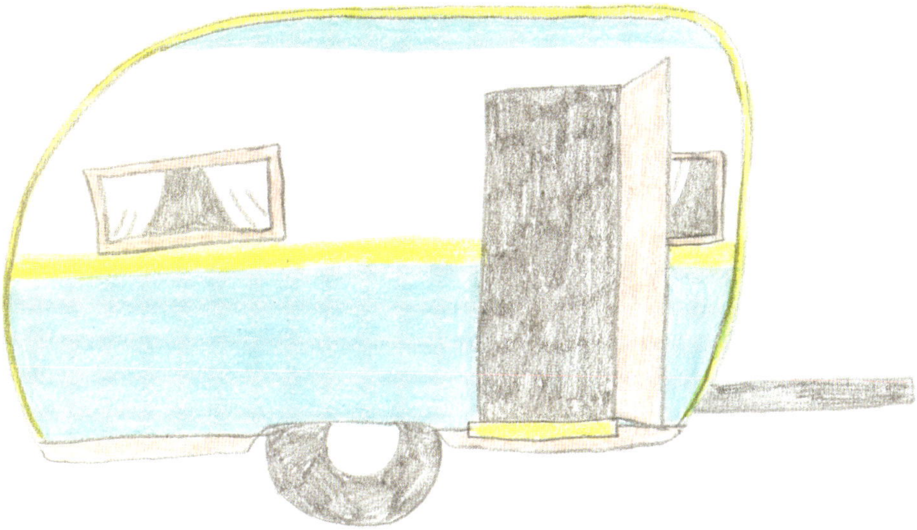

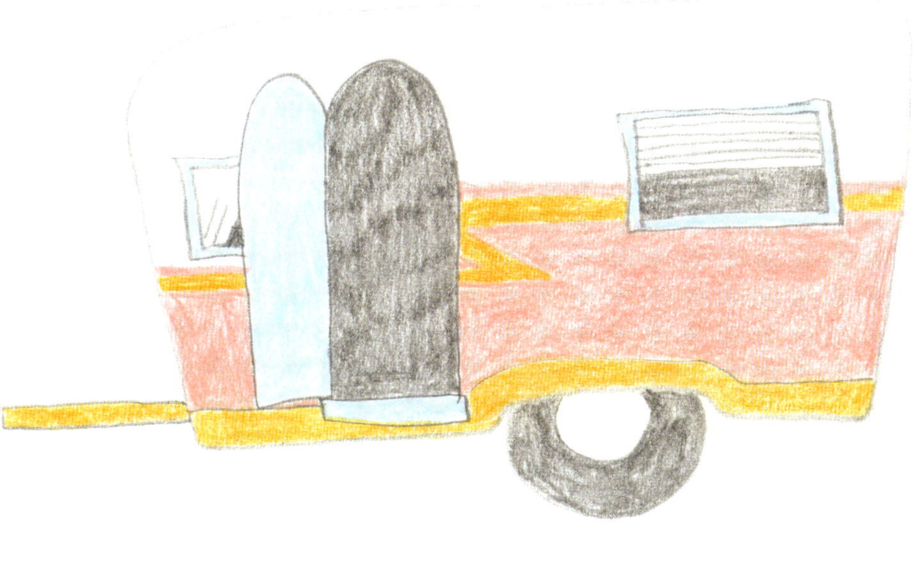

What are some other colors and designs that might work well on a camper? Try a 1960s-inspired color palette, or come up with something totally off-the-wall and original!

NATURE & ITS FURRY FRIENDS

Being out in nature is one of the most inspiring things you can do. Nature can encompass many different scenarios, including a bustling city park, a serene hike, a lush greenhouse, and camping in various seasons. Because I spend a lot of time drawing architectural urban scenes, I like to change things up by drawing nature scenes. Drawing nature reminds me to keep a loose hand and an organic look to my artwork.

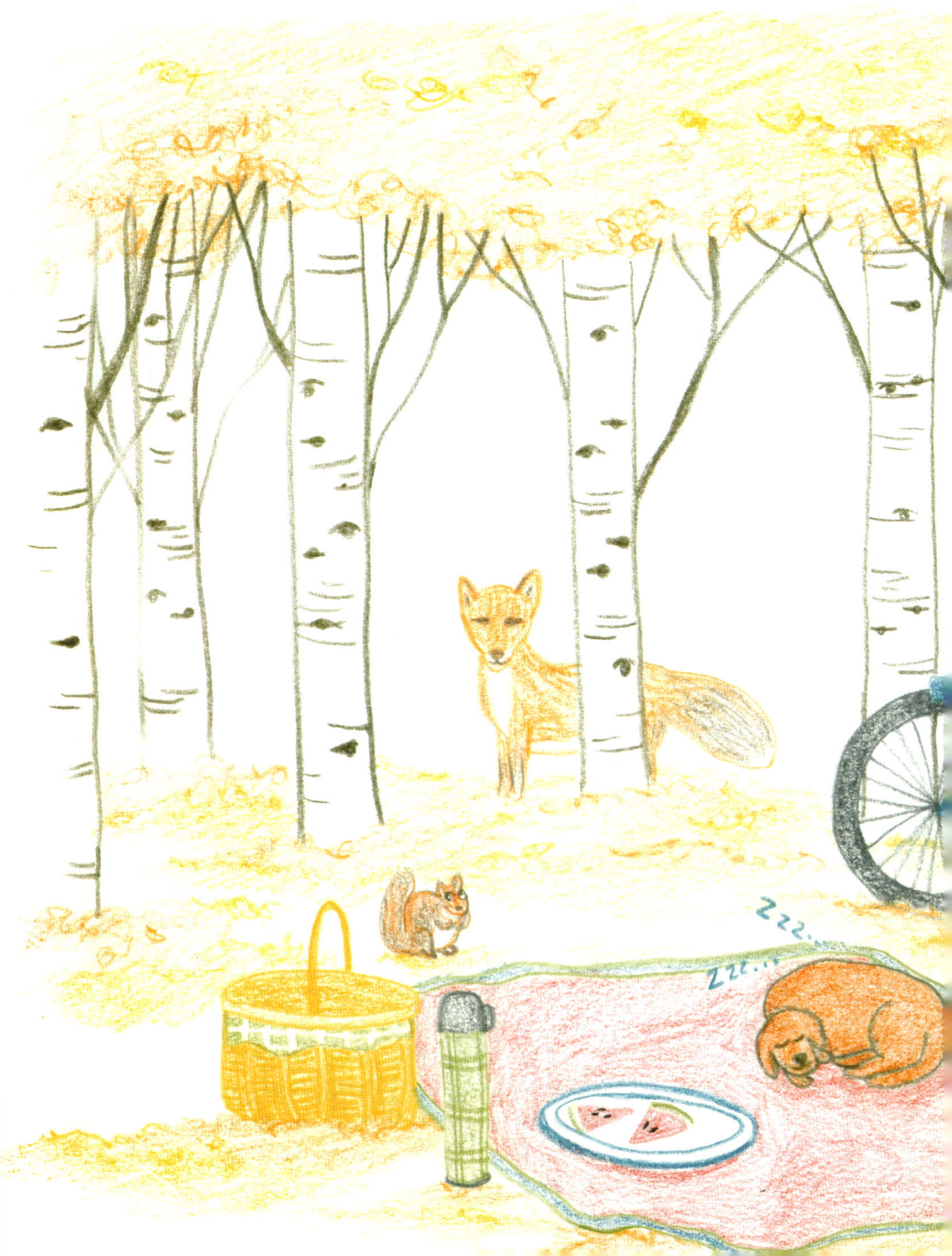

It is important to remember that while you are drawing out in nature, you do not have to draw every detail of everything you see. Nature is boundless, and if you attempt to draw every single leaf, branch, and blade of grass, you will tire yourself out and lose the essence of what you are trying to capture. Take a moment to soak in your scenery and decide which of nature's features you'd like to emphasize in your drawing.

First, let's start by learning how to draw a couple of animals—they are adorable and can add a lot of character to a drawing.

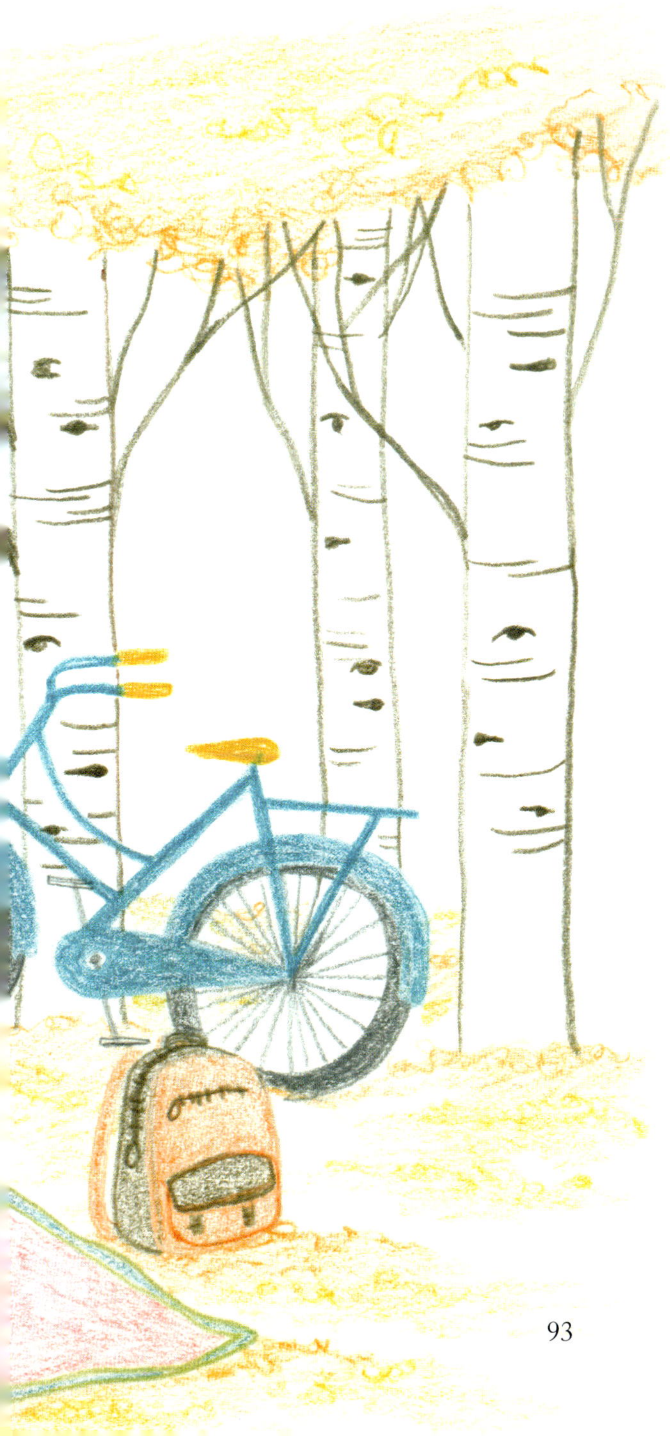

SQUIRREL

STEP 1

When drawing animals, I sketch out their general shapes with a #2 pencil. This helps me to keep the animal's proportions lifelike. If you do not see a squirrel, use photographs as a reference. Sketch out the body, head, and tail of your squirrel.

To keep proportion, notice the size of the shapes in comparison to one another. For instance, I noticed that the squirrel's head is about a third of the size of its body, and its tail is the tallest feature.

STEP 2

Lightly erase the lines you just drew, leaving a faint outline that you can trace. Using a midtone color (not the darkest color and not the lightest color of the squirrel), draw the squirrel's arms, legs, and ears. Then complete your squirrel's outline using your sketched lines from the previous step. Lightly mark areas of the squirrel that you want to maintain white—for instance, the belly and around the eyes.

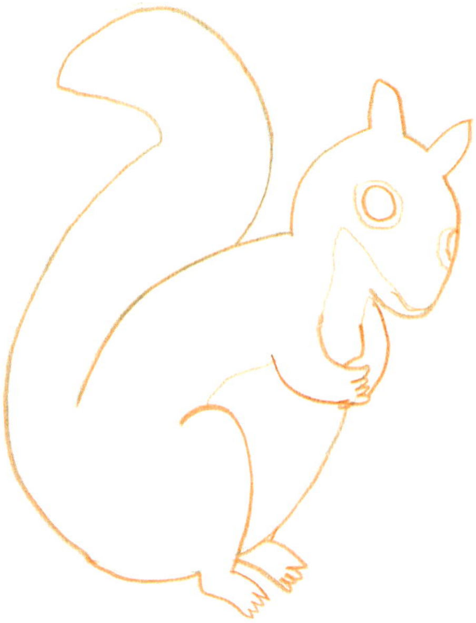

STEP 3

Continue to use the midtone color. Draw hash marks for the fur where appropriate. When making the hash marks, follow the natural curves of the squirrel's body. Squirrels have shorter fur, so use shorter hash marks.

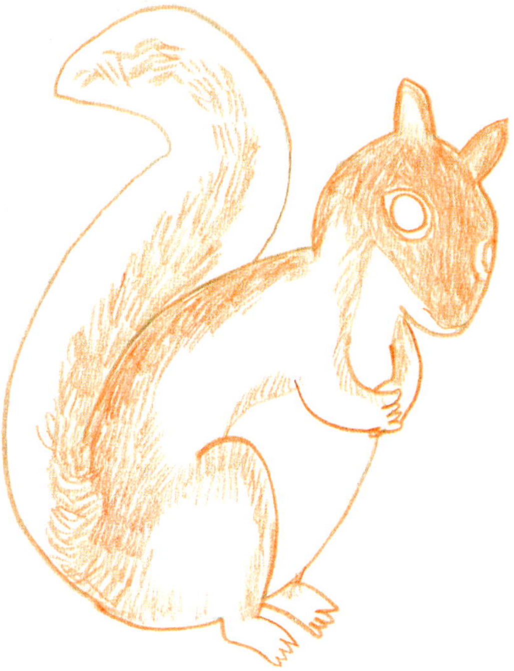

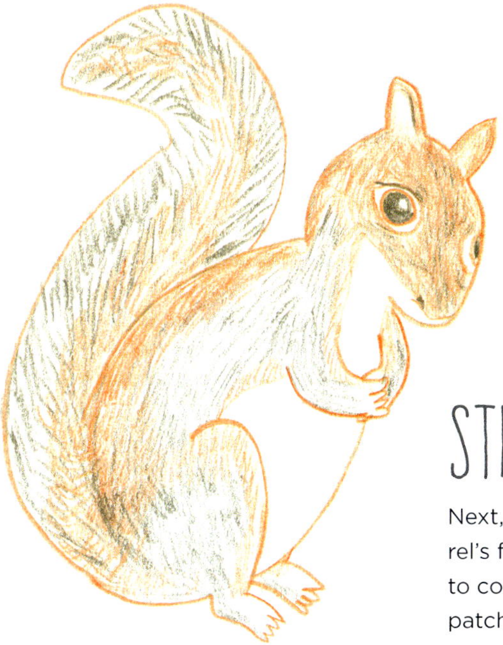

STEP 4

Next, using a darker color for the squirrel's fur, continue drawing hash marks to complete the fur for the darker patches. Also, use this color to fill in your squirrel's eyes and to make little nostrils! How cute is that?

FOX

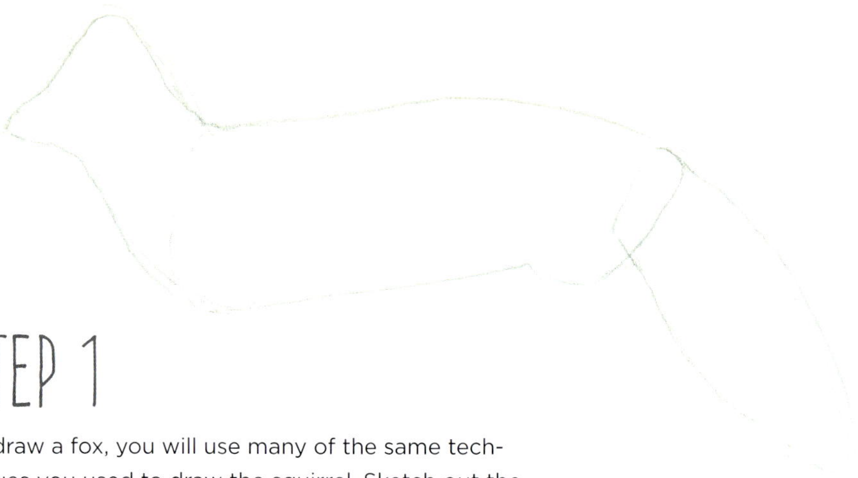

STEP 1

To draw a fox, you will use many of the same techniques you used to draw the squirrel. Sketch out the body, head, and tail of the fox with a regular pencil. I was surprised when I realized that a fox's tail is almost as big as its body!

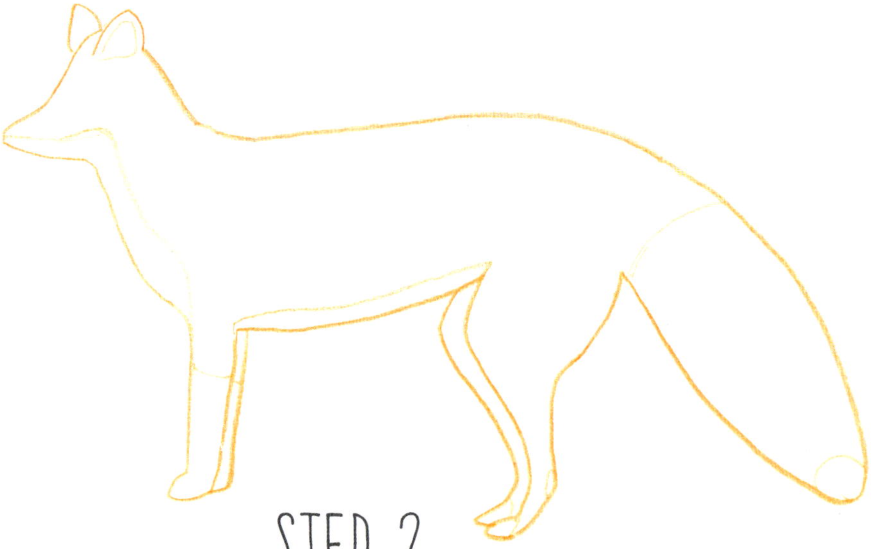

STEP 2

Gently erase the graphite lines, and use the fox's midtone color to draw the limbs and ears. Then complete the outline of the fox's body. You do not need to draw exactly according to your original sketch. If you notice something off, change it. Then lightly mark the areas that will remain white.

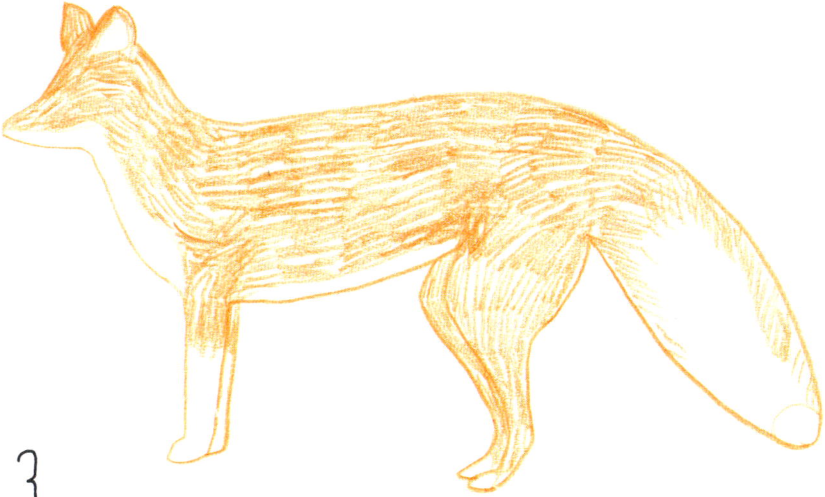

STEP 3

Use the same midtone color to fill in the appropriate areas. A fox's fur is longer than that of a squirrel, so use longer hash marks when filling in the fur. Mimic the curves of the fox's body.

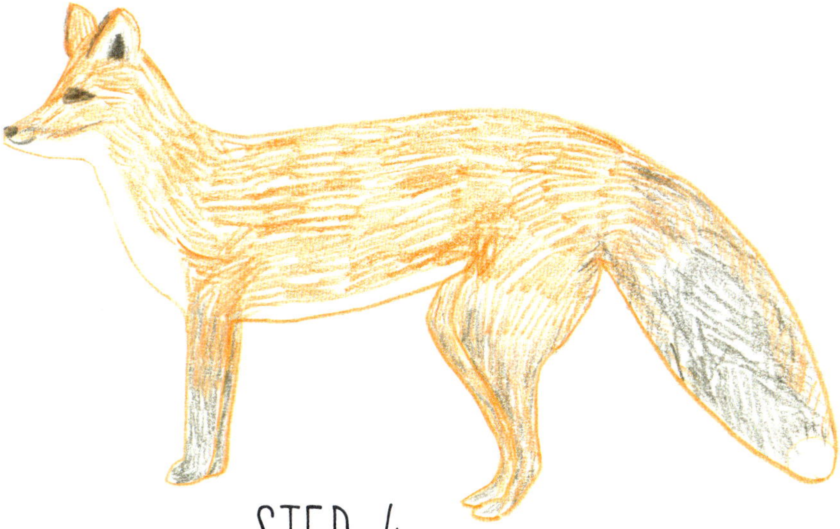

STEP 4

Finally, use a darker brown or gray color to complete the dark areas of fur. Add detail with this color to the fox's ears, eyes, nose, and mouth.

GRASS

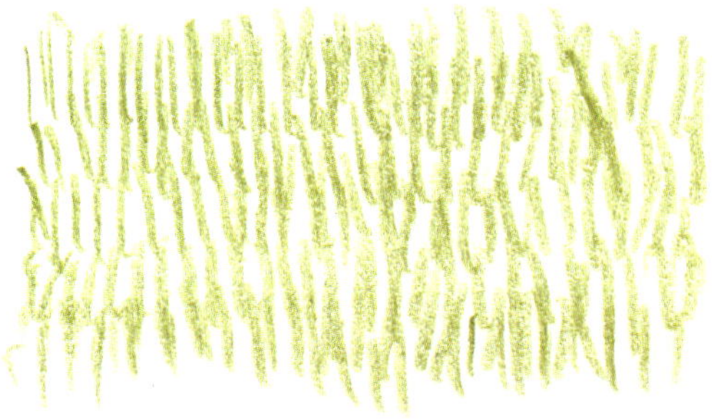

STEP 1

Drawing grass is super simple. Use short, vertical hash marks with a green color.

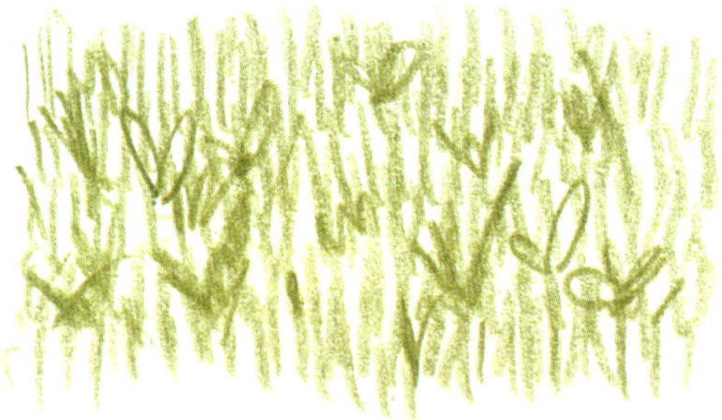

STEP 2

Next, draw in a few stray lines and weeds to add interest and nonconformity to your patch of grass. If you find this is not dark enough for your liking, shade the whole patch of grass with the same green color, but use a lighter hand so you do not lose details from your hatching.

BIRCH TREE

Birch trees are my favorites because of their stark contrast between white bark and dark details. These features also happen to make birch trees quite enjoyable and easy to draw!

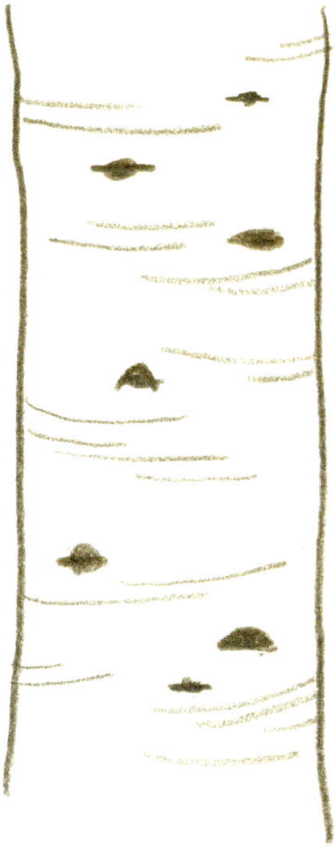

STEP 1

Draw two imperfect, parallel, vertical lines for the trunk with a very dark brown color. Then draw some knots in the tree's bark by making small circles and ovals with a thick line through, above, or below the circles or ovals. Draw many curved, horizontal lines in the bark. Curving the lines creates the illusion of a round trunk.

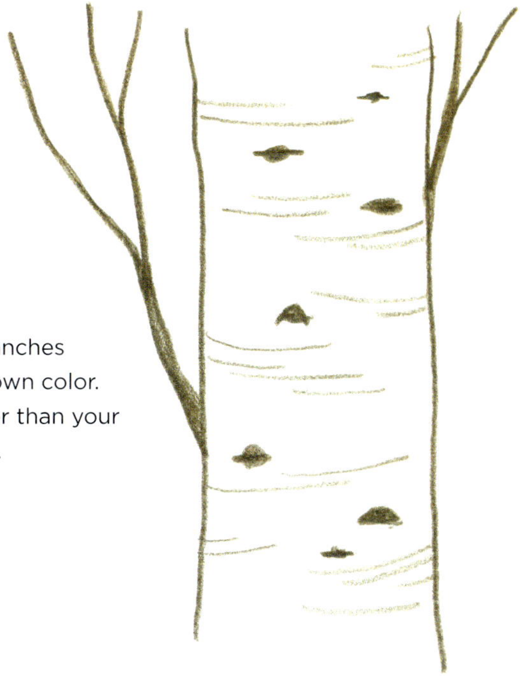

STEP 2

Next, draw in some branches with the same dark brown color. Make these lines thicker than your curved horizontal lines.

CREATING THE ILLUSION OF MANY LEAVES

Each tree has many thousands of leaves, but you don't need to draw them all! As we discussed earlier, it is often better not to draw every single detail you see. Instead, focus your attention on accentuating specific areas of the scene that you like best. I love creating the illusion of leaves because I get to use some techniques that result in an impressionistic look.

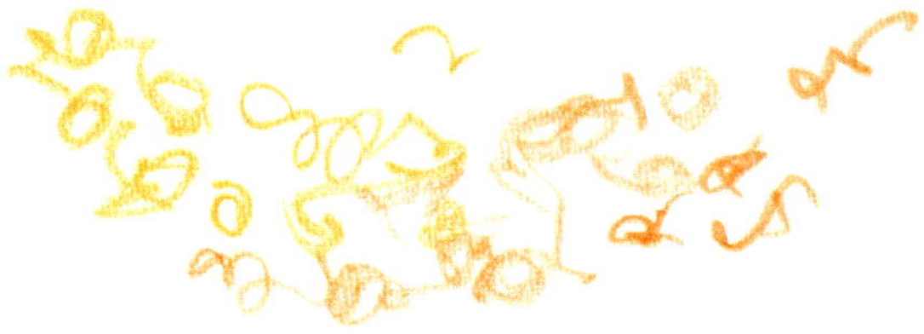

STEP 1

After choosing your colors for the leaves, draw some loose, curving, and scribbling lines on your page around where the batches of leaves end. Use heavy pressure here.

Sometimes a really lovely scene can be somewhat overwhelming because of how many options there are to capture in your drawing. Before committing to a larger, final drawing, I often like to make little thumbnail sketches of possible compositions. These are done very quickly and without pressure. This is also a great way to test out a color palette!

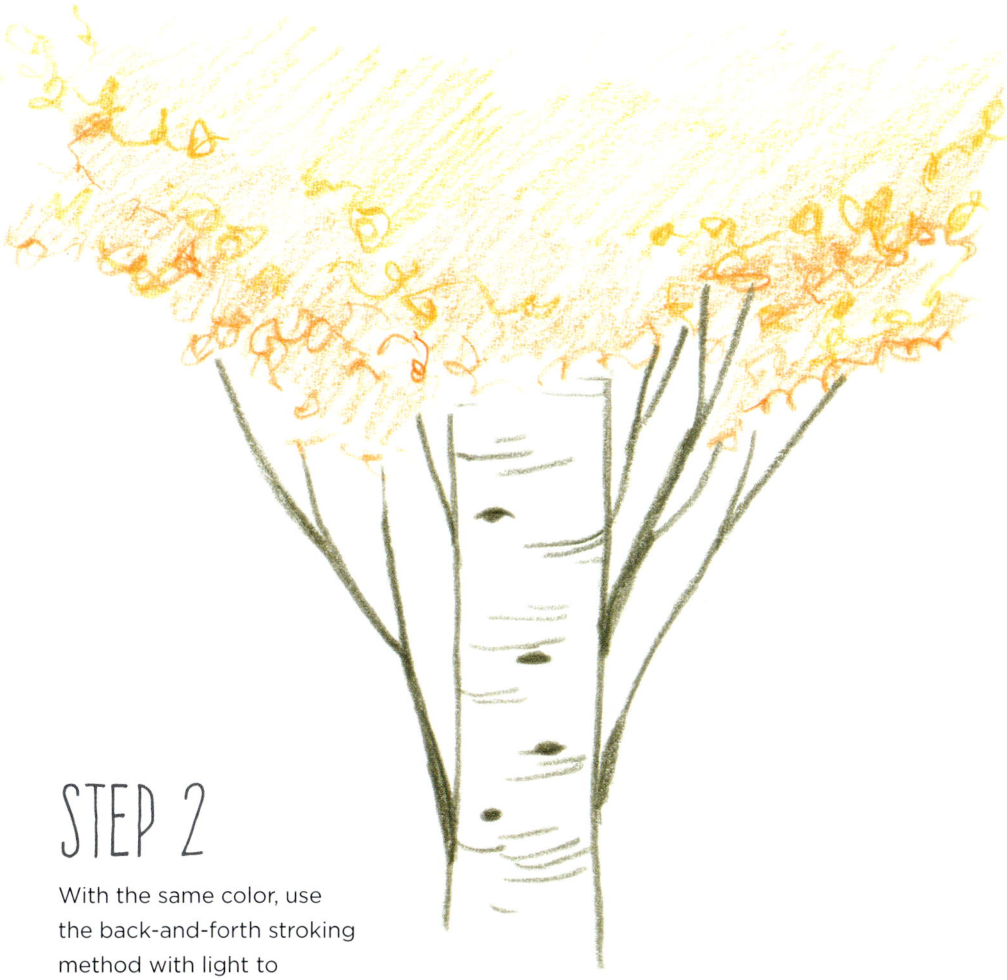

STEP 2

With the same color, use the back-and-forth stroking method with light to moderate pressure to fill in the rest of the leaf area.

Be random with where you draw details on trees and not too symmetrical. Very few things in nature are symmetrical.

ARCHITECTURE & CITYSCAPES

Cityscapes are among my all-time favorite subjects to draw. I love the geometry of architecture and the energy of city life. Because of these two factors in particular, I believe architectural drawings can elicit much emotion. Much of the artwork that I create in my spare time incorporates urban architecture in one way or another. I find the straight lines and angles soothing to draw.

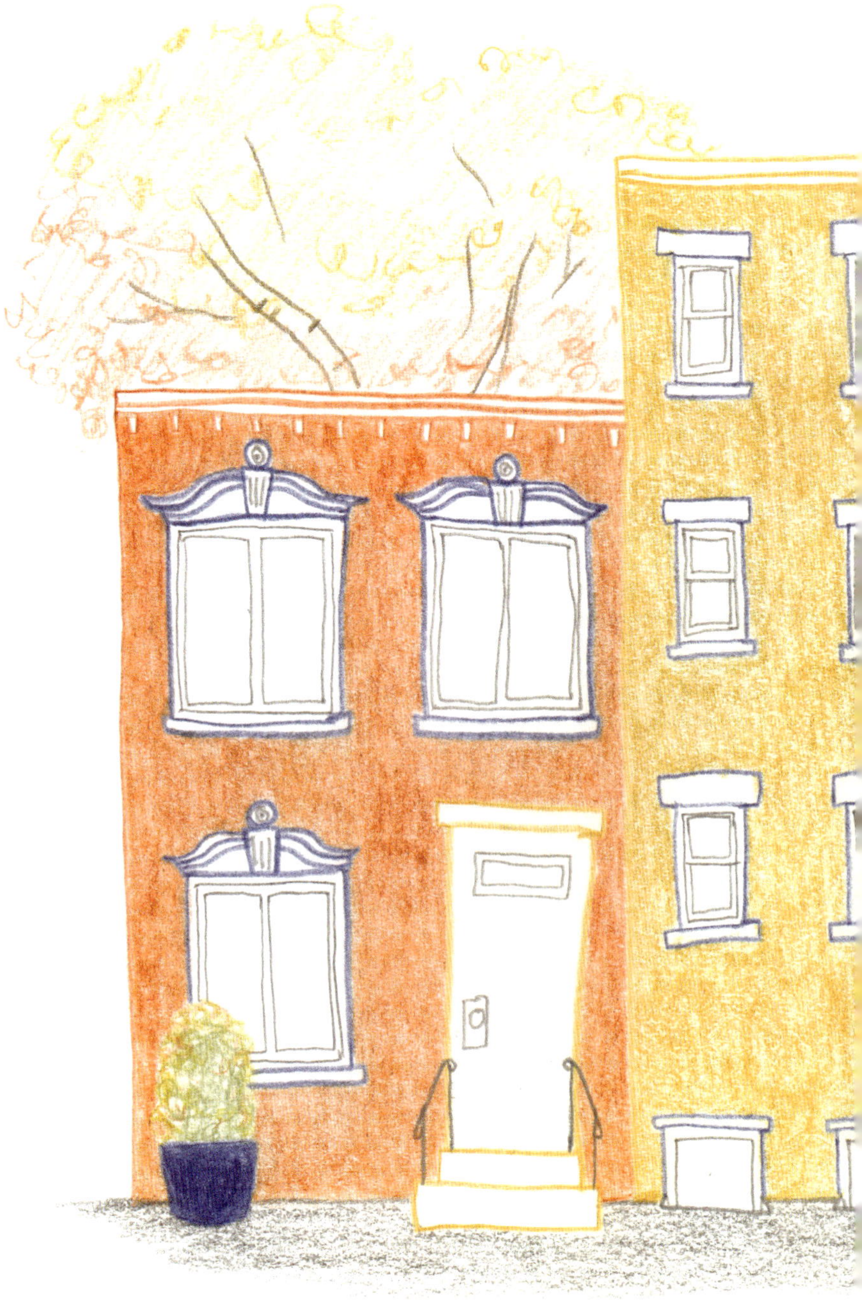

In this chapter, I will guide you through a few observational exercises to develop an awareness of the various architectural elements around you. Specifically, you will sketch out some examples of stairs, windows, and cornices. Let's put your colored pencils to the test with the exercises in this chapter!

To start, go for a walk around a small town or city block if possible. Pay close attention to the buildings as you walk, and notice the little details that make each building unique. Consider color palette, shapes, and proportions. You can start the drawing exercises while out and about if you have your sketchbook in tow, or you can snap a couple photos to use as reference when you draw at home.

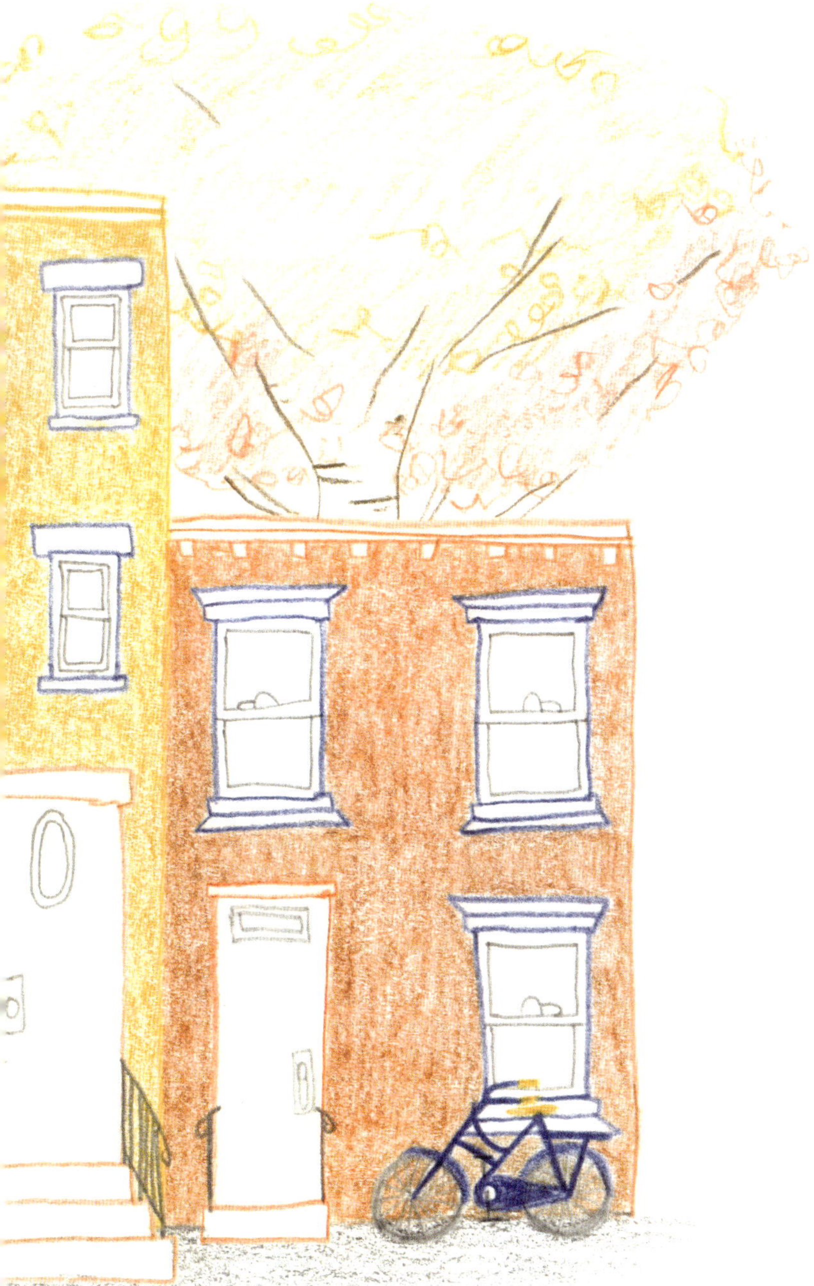

STAIRS

Stairs are very easy to draw straight on. Although steps in a staircase are typically the same size, perspective makes them appear to get smaller as they recede from the viewer.

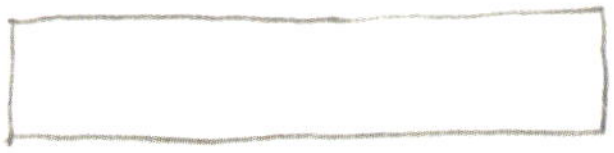

STEP 1

Since the bottom step is closest to the viewer, it will be the largest when you draw it. Start with a rectangle for the first step.

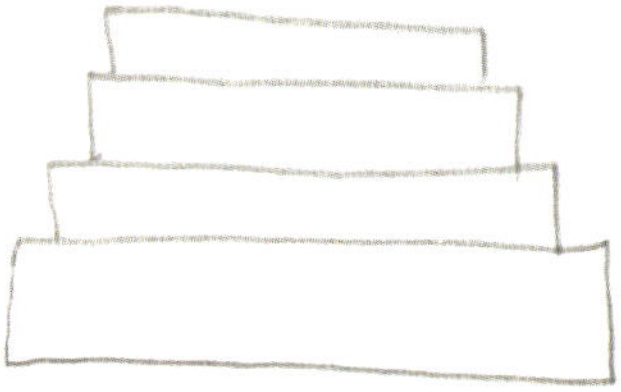

STEP 2

Add as many steps as you'd like by drawing more rectangles in decreasing size on top of the bottom step.

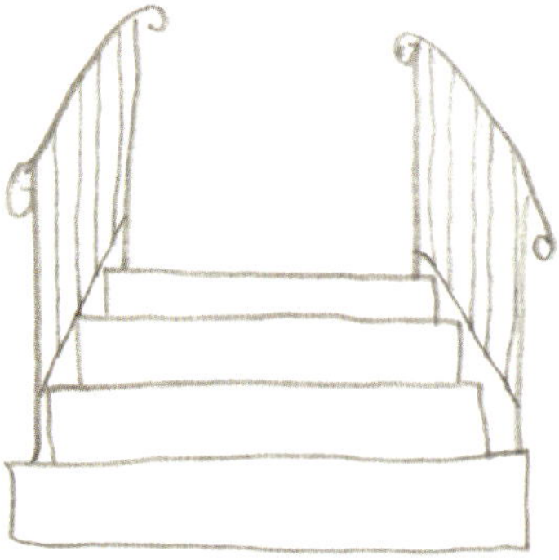

STEP 3

Add interest to your staircase with railings.

WINDOWS

Windows are usually composed of rectangles inside of rectangles. They tend to differ in style with their adornments and handles.

STEP 1

Sketch some windows.

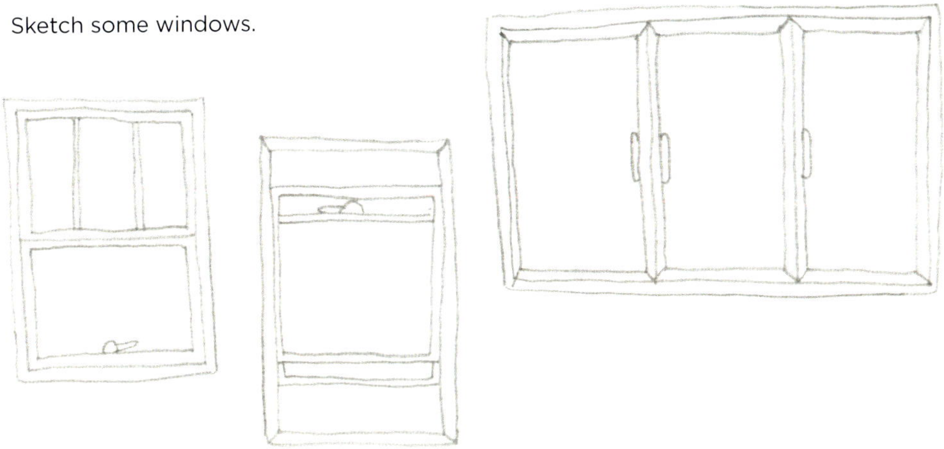

STEP 2

Add details to your windows, such as panes, locks, frames, and sills.

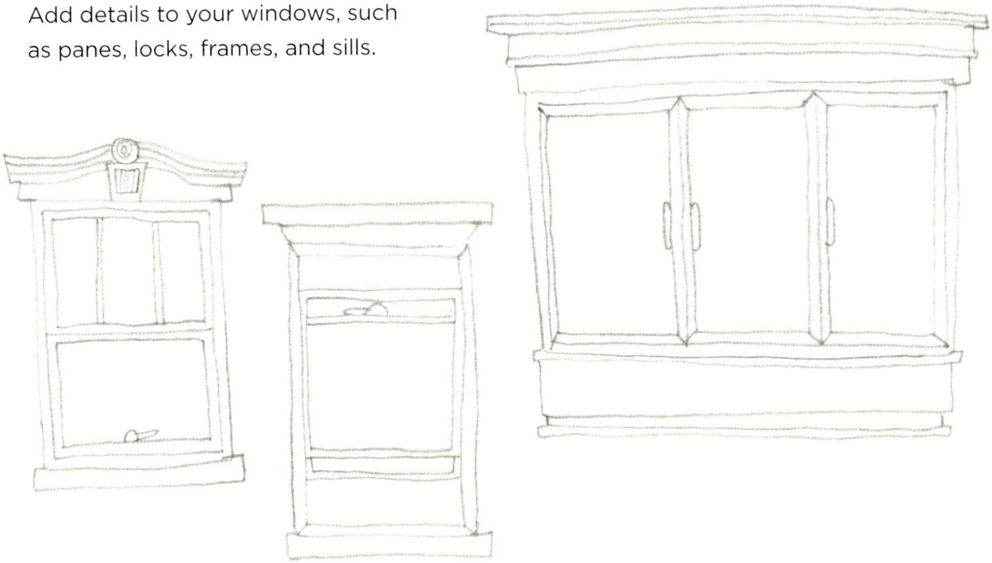

CORNICES

Cornices are my favorite part of a building to draw. Cornices are the ornamental or decorative features you see on the tops of walls. They are often the most intricately decorated part of a building's facade.

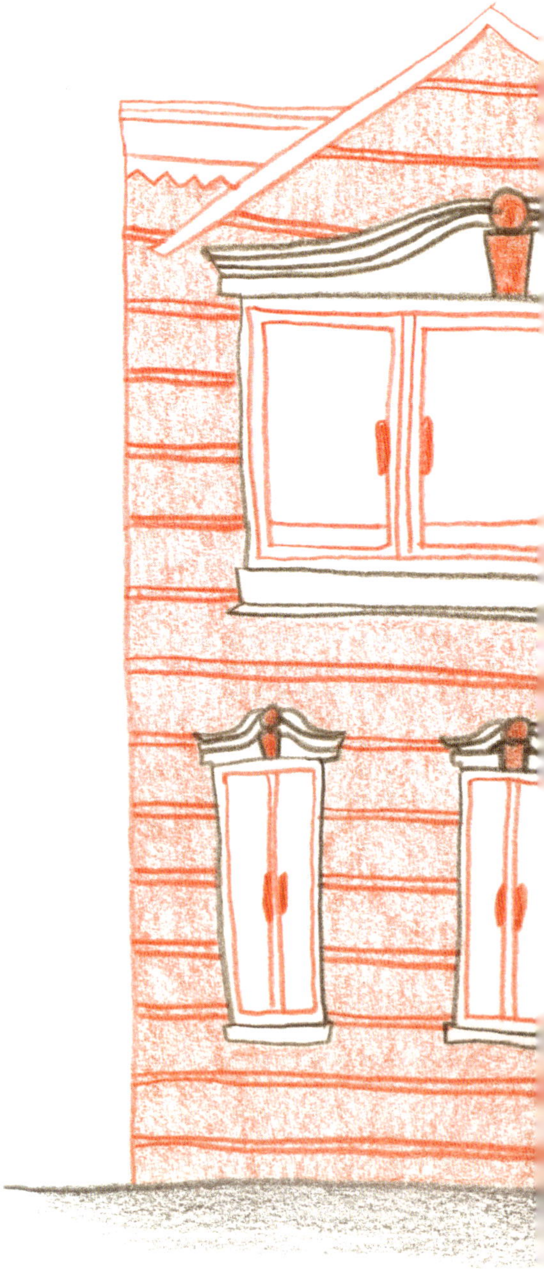

STEP 1

Draw the straight line of the roof, and work from there.

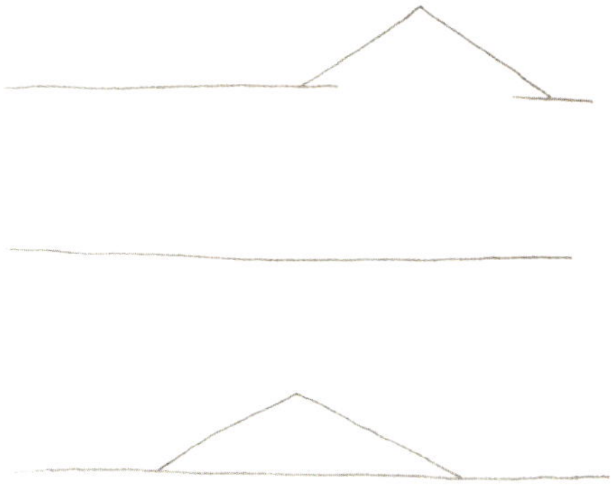

STEP 2

Experiment with some designs from your imagination!

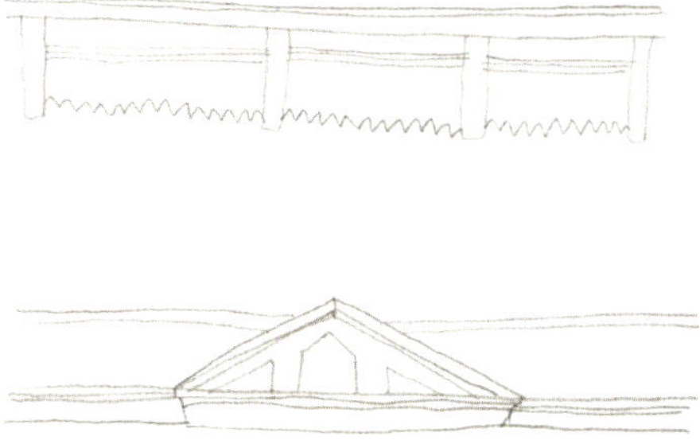

BUILDING DETAILS

Starting with the basic outline of a building, you basically have a big rectangle. How you spruce up this rectangle is your choice! With the components explored in this chapter, mix and match as you please to create buildings. Keep in mind that you never have to draw exactly what is in front of you. If you liked the color of one building but the cornice of another, create a building combining these two attributes!

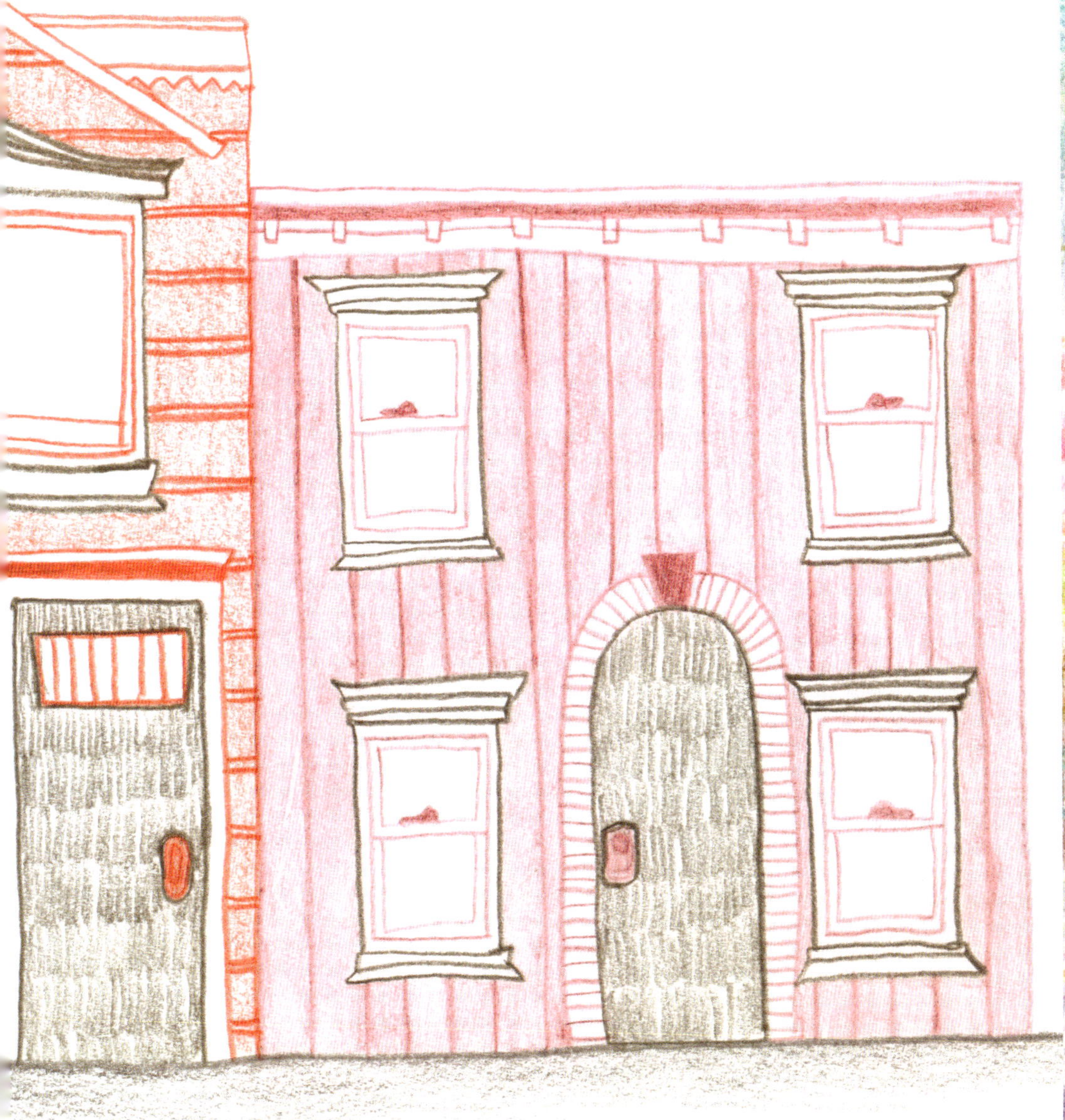

COFFEE COMFORTS

A café is a wonderful location to spur inspiration for your artwork. Being in a space filled with people moving around, socializing, and caffeinating themselves naturally encourages a similar kind of energy in the observer. I love bringing my art supplies to cafés and capturing this unique energy. Not only is it creatively invigorating to be in the atmosphere of a coffeehouse, it also provides a plethora of interesting subject matters to draw!

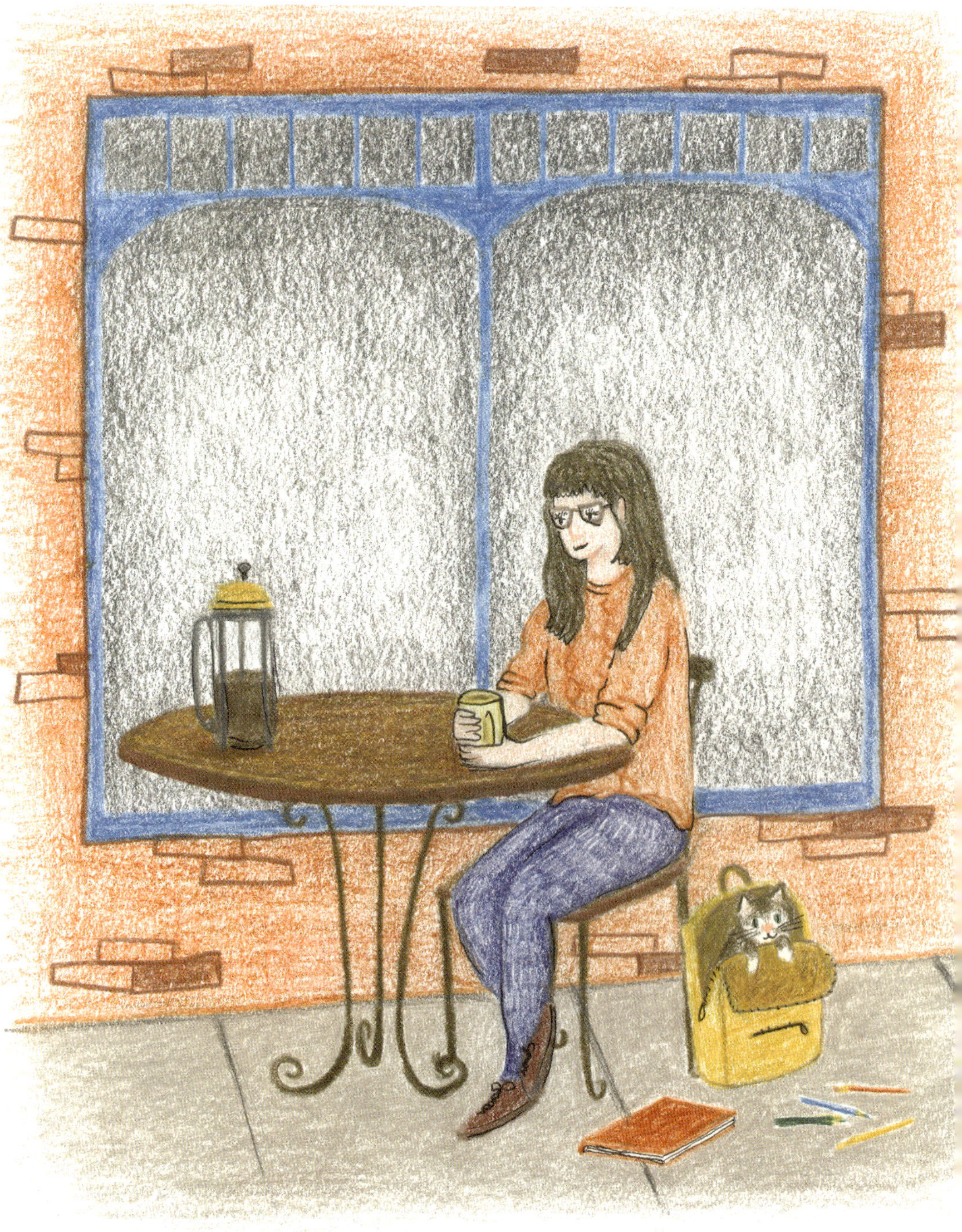

CROISSANT

STEP 1

To start the shape of a croissant, create a soft, crescent moon shape using mustard or another warm yellow color, and then add a straight line between the two tips of the crescent. Apply light pressure for this part.

STEP 2

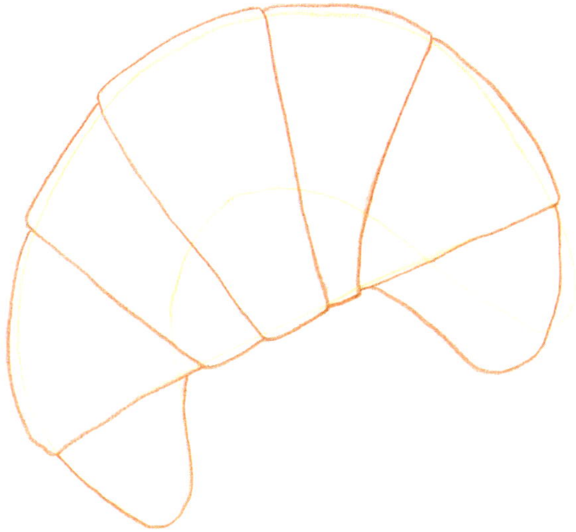

Croissants are made by rolling the dough up on top of itself, which creates layers with different heights on the pastry. Mark off these sections of the croissant with a brownish-orange color.

STEP 3

Next, using moderate pressure, fill in these shapes with the same orange color and your choice of fill techniques (see page 14).

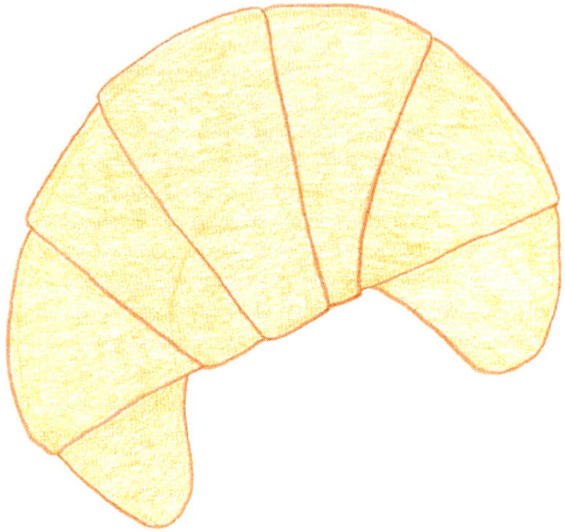

For drawings that incorporate light and dark colors, lay down the lighter color first.

STEP 4

Finally, let's toast these flaky, buttery croissants! Beginning at the center of each section, shade with the same brownish-orange color, and lighten up as you move toward the outside of each section. For even darker areas, add a brown shade. Add some darkness to the creases between layers. I made the highest section of the croissant lighter than the tips because it is closer to the viewer and less crispy than the ends. Are you as hungry as I am now?

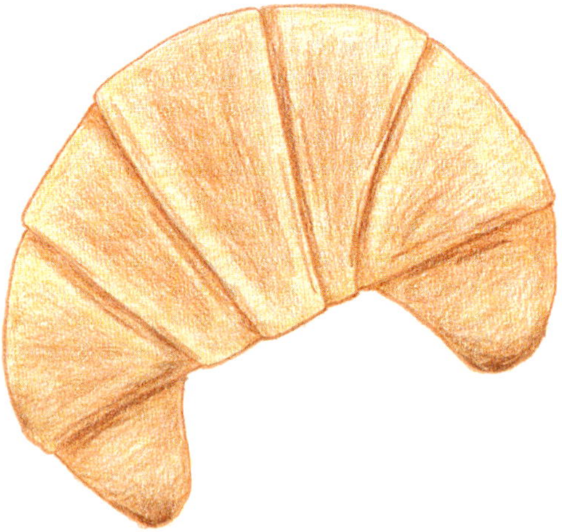

FRENCH PRESS

STEP 1

With a gray colored pencil, draw a rectangle with a rounded bottom using heavy pressure. This will be the glass vessel of the press.

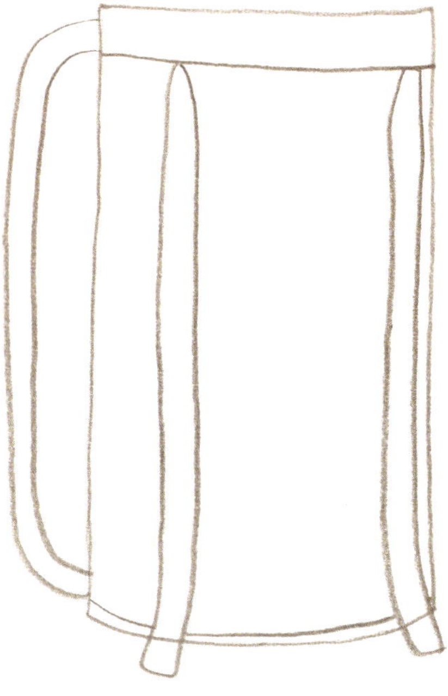

STEP 2

Next, draw the legs and handle of the French press.

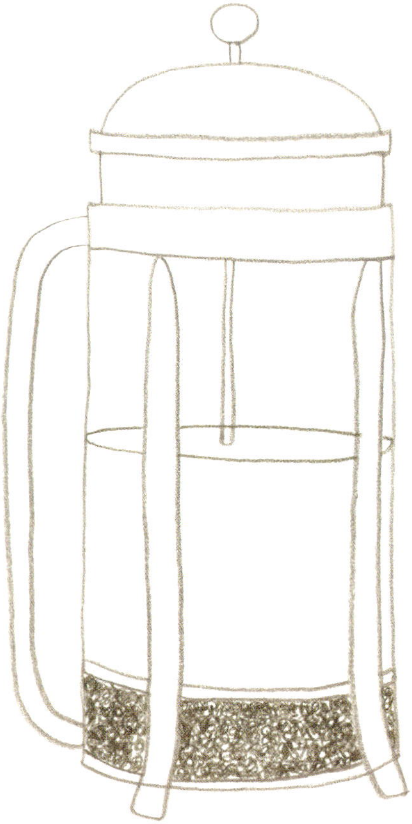

STEP 3

Draw the lid and plunger of the French press and the water line. The water line is the top of where the coffee will fill your French press. Draw the water line in the shape of an oval. Then draw the bottom of the plunger, and add the coffee grounds below by drawing small scribbles with a dark brown pencil.

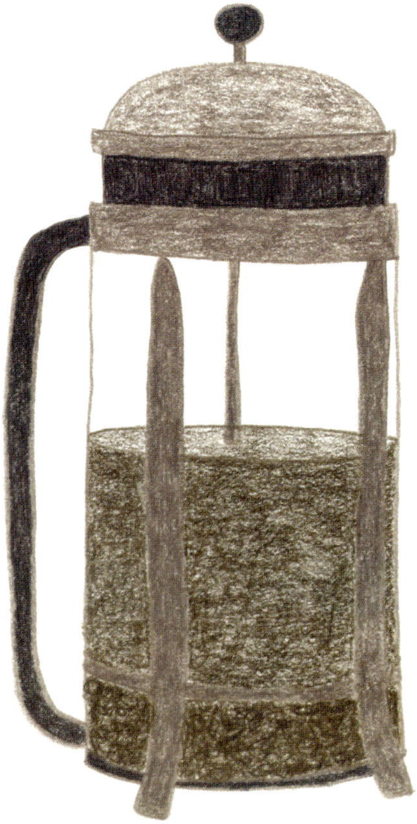

STEP 4

Color in your French press with the color of your choice. I opted for a more classic black and silver/gray French press with dark roast coffee. Color in your coffee with a shade of brown, and don't forget to go over the area with the grounds!

COFFEE MUG

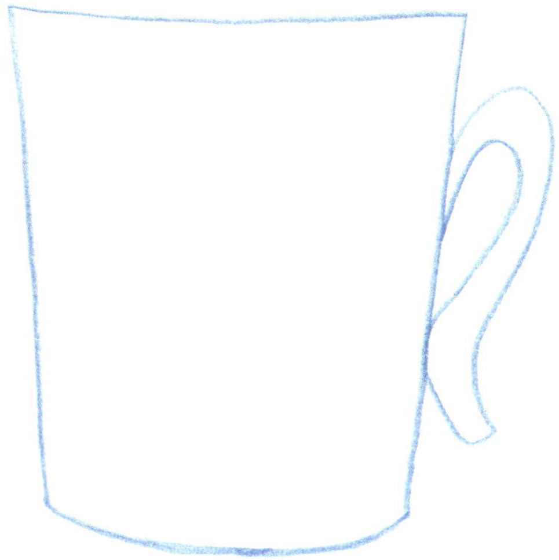

STEP 1

Draw a simple rectangular shape in a color that makes you happy. What color would your ideal coffee mug be? Then add the handle! Draw a very simple handle or one with more flourish.

STEP 2

On a scrap piece of paper or in the dedicated patterns section of your sketchbook, test out some patterns using your mug color and at least one other color. Which is your favorite? Transfer that pattern onto your mug!

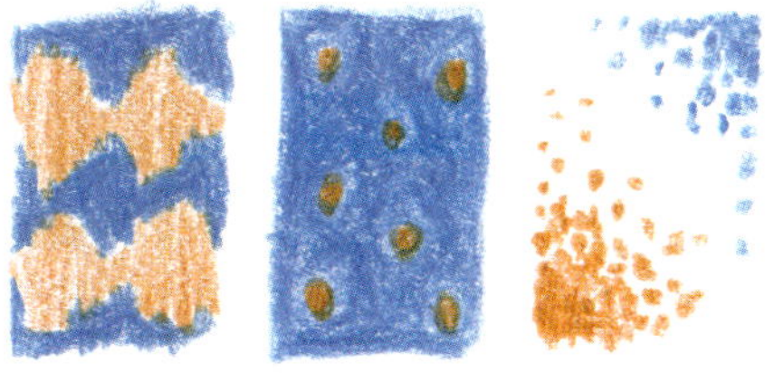

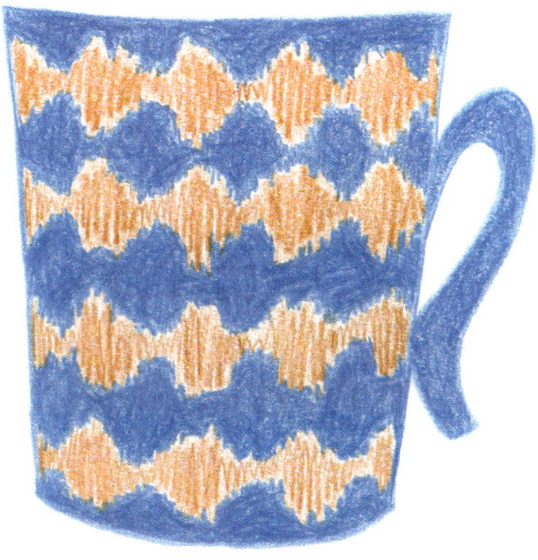

TRAVEL SKETCHING

Traveling is one of the most inspiring activities a person can do. When traveling, you are exposed each day to new situations and cultures. I often find myself overflowing with inspiration and creativity while traveling. Depending on your schedule during your adventure, it's great to find some time to sit down and sketch your surroundings. However, if you are busy or wish to absorb as much as you can of your experience, quick photographs snapped on your phone or camera can serve as an excellent reference later.

This chapter will focus on learning how to use guidelines of composition and perspective to create interesting drawings.

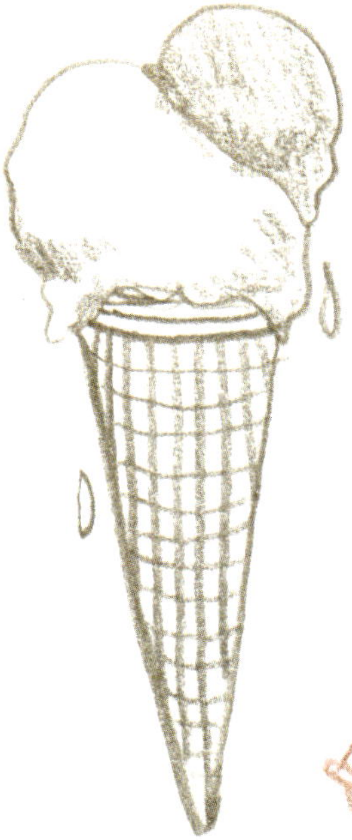

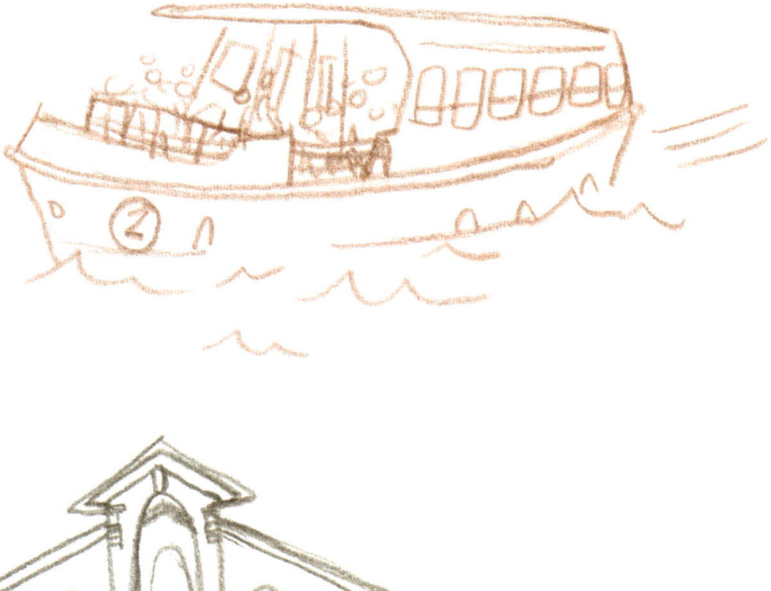

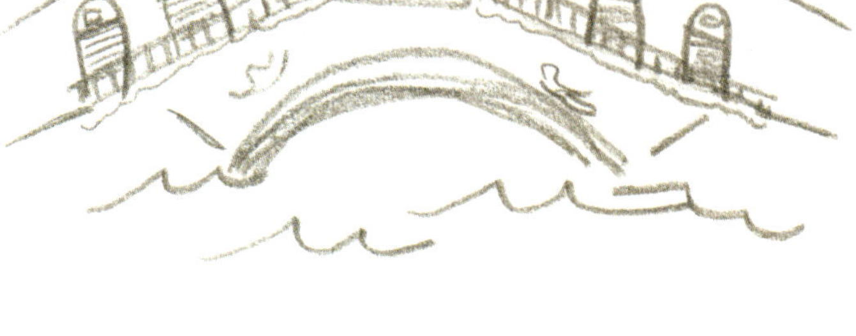

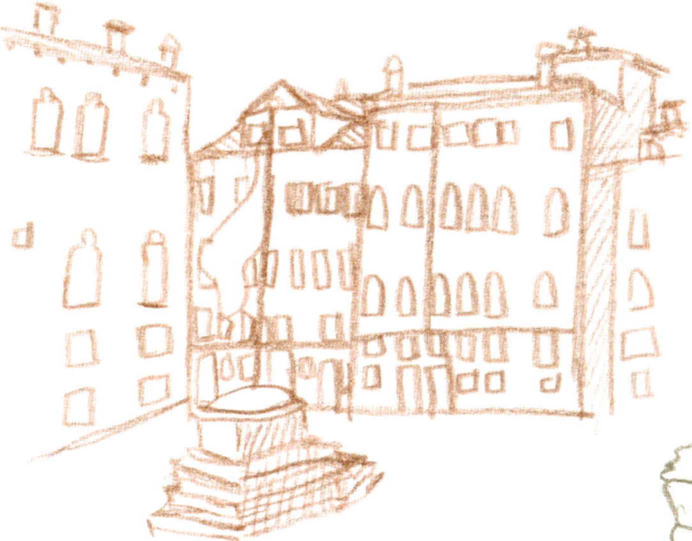

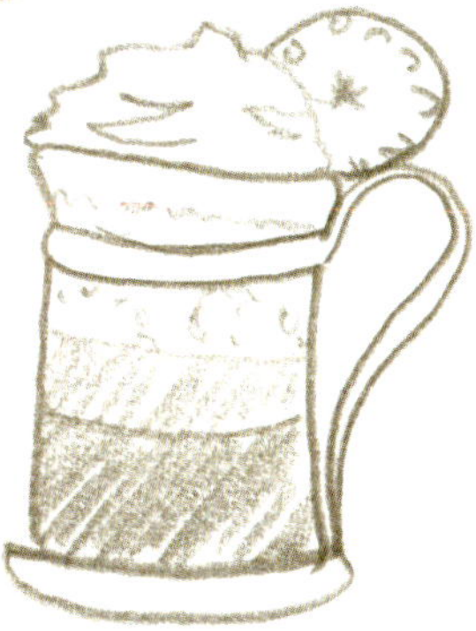

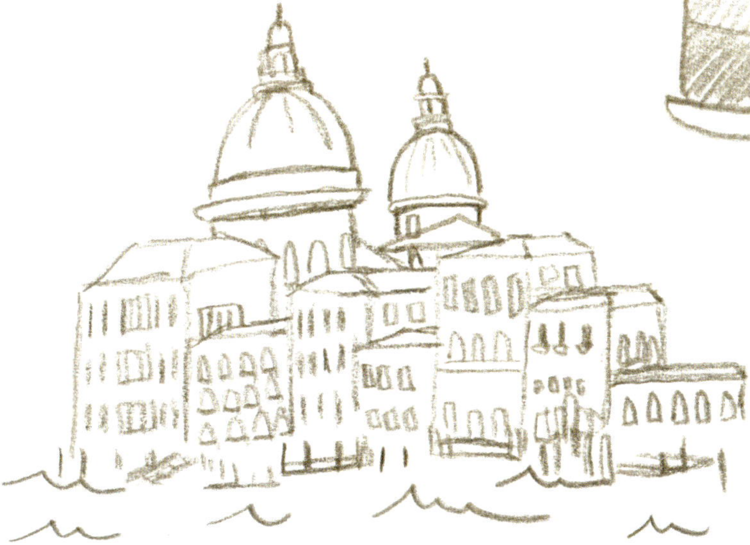

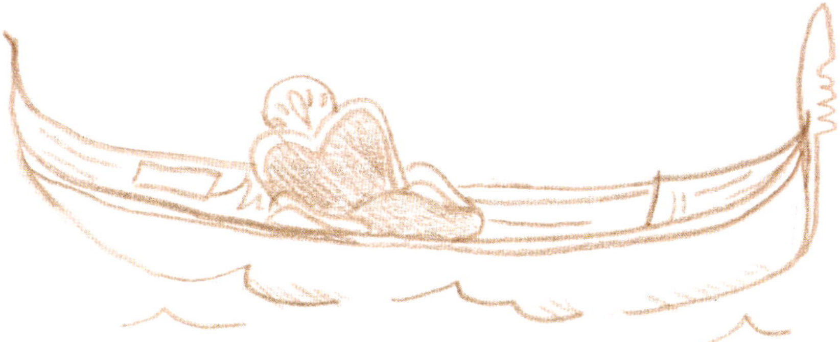

RULE OF THIRDS

When it comes to creating a pleasing composition, I frequently refer to the "rule of thirds." This means that the subject of emphasis in your piece will be positioned a third of the way from either side of your paper, horizontally or vertically. Furthermore, if you look at your paper as being broken down into thirds both horizontally and vertically, you can position a subject anywhere these lines intersect.

STEP 1

In your sketchbook or on a piece of scrap paper, divide the page into thirds by drawing two vertical lines. Try to make these as equidistant as you can.

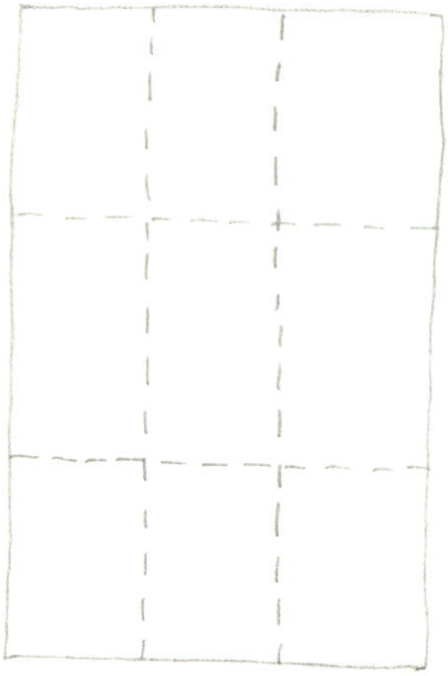

STEP 2

Then draw two horizontal lines. Your page should be divided into nine equal sections. Use the rule of thirds to help you position your sketches.

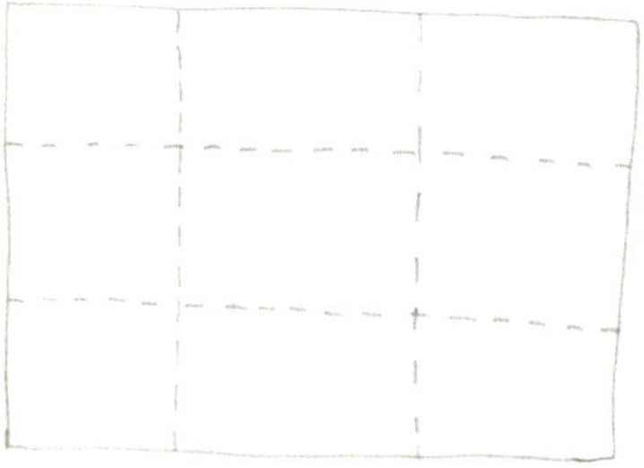

PERSPECTIVE OR FINDING THE HORIZON

Perspective can help your drawings achieve a greater sense of depth. This sense of depth is important when drawing a scene that recedes into the distance.

One of the most helpful things you can do to create perspective in your piece is to determine the horizon line.

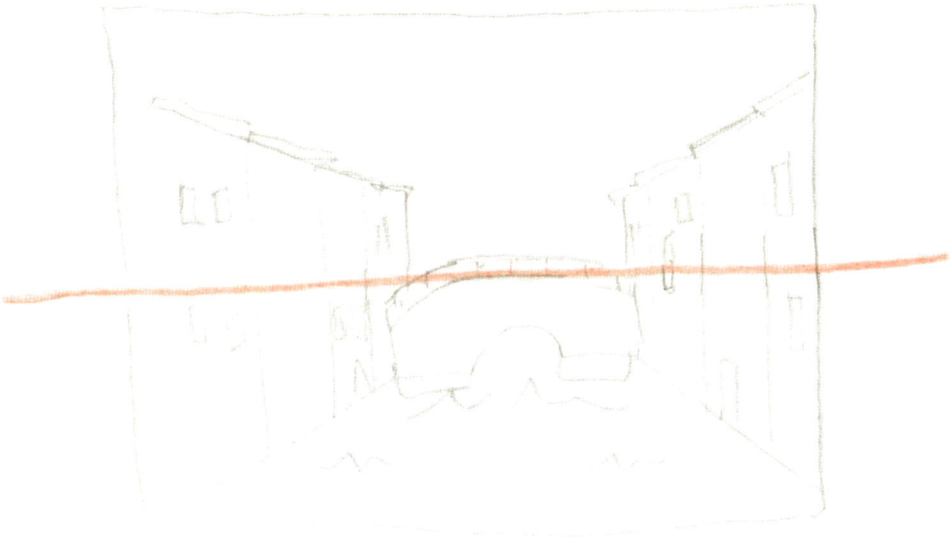

Notice how the roofs of the buildings slope down and the bottoms of the buildings slope up toward the horizon line. Any horizontal lines drawn close to the horizon line will be parallel or close to parallel to it. The farther away from the horizon line, the more angled your lines will be.

The horizon line will always be at your eye level when viewing a scene in person or at the level of your camera lens when taking a photograph.

WAVES

Having spent my residency in Venice, Italy, I was surrounded every day by the beautiful blue-green water of the canals and the Adriatic Sea. Here I have shown a few different ways to draw water with your colored pencils, depending on how smooth the water is.

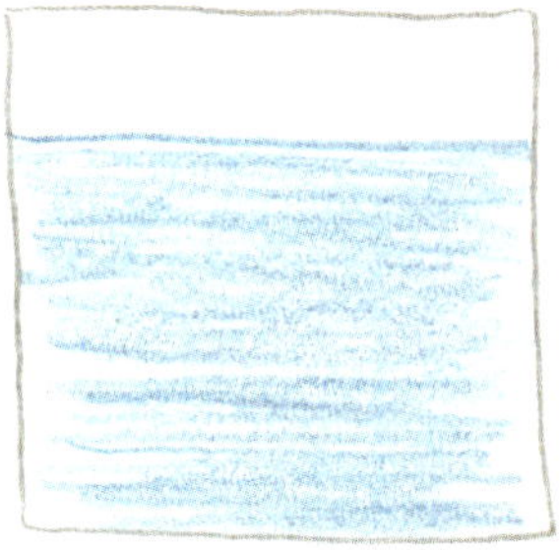

SMOOTH

Use hard pressure to draw a horizontal line where the water meets the land or sky. Then, using varying pressure, draw more horizontal lines to fill in the water.

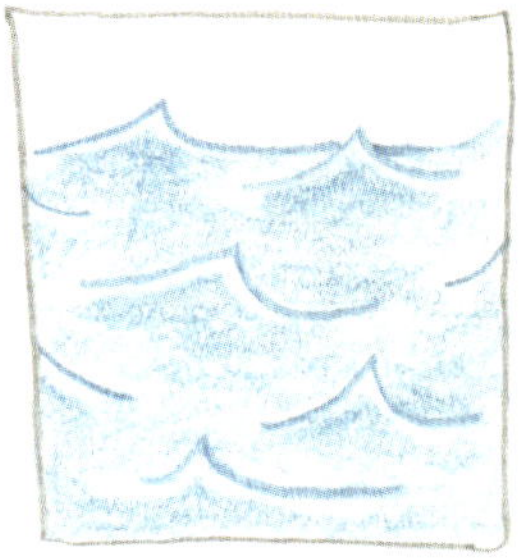

WAVY

Draw peaks for the crests of the waves. Then draw in the horizontal line where the water ends. Using varying pressure, create a gradient of color by increasing pressure (and therefore saturation) as you get toward the tip of each crest.

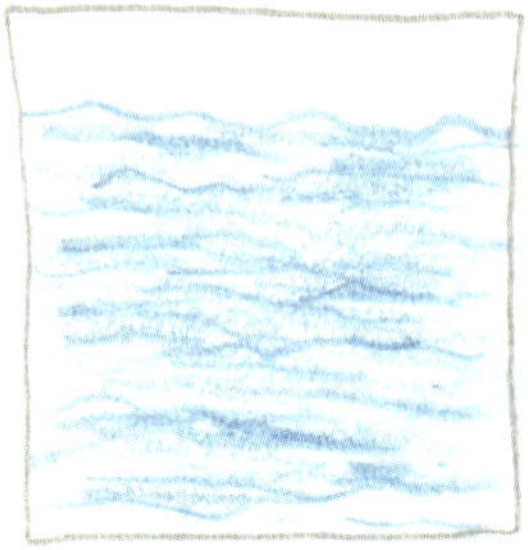

CHOPPY

Draw wavy lines with hard pressure throughout the space where you want your water to be. Then use light and moderate pressure to make loose horizontal lines to fill in the rest of the space.

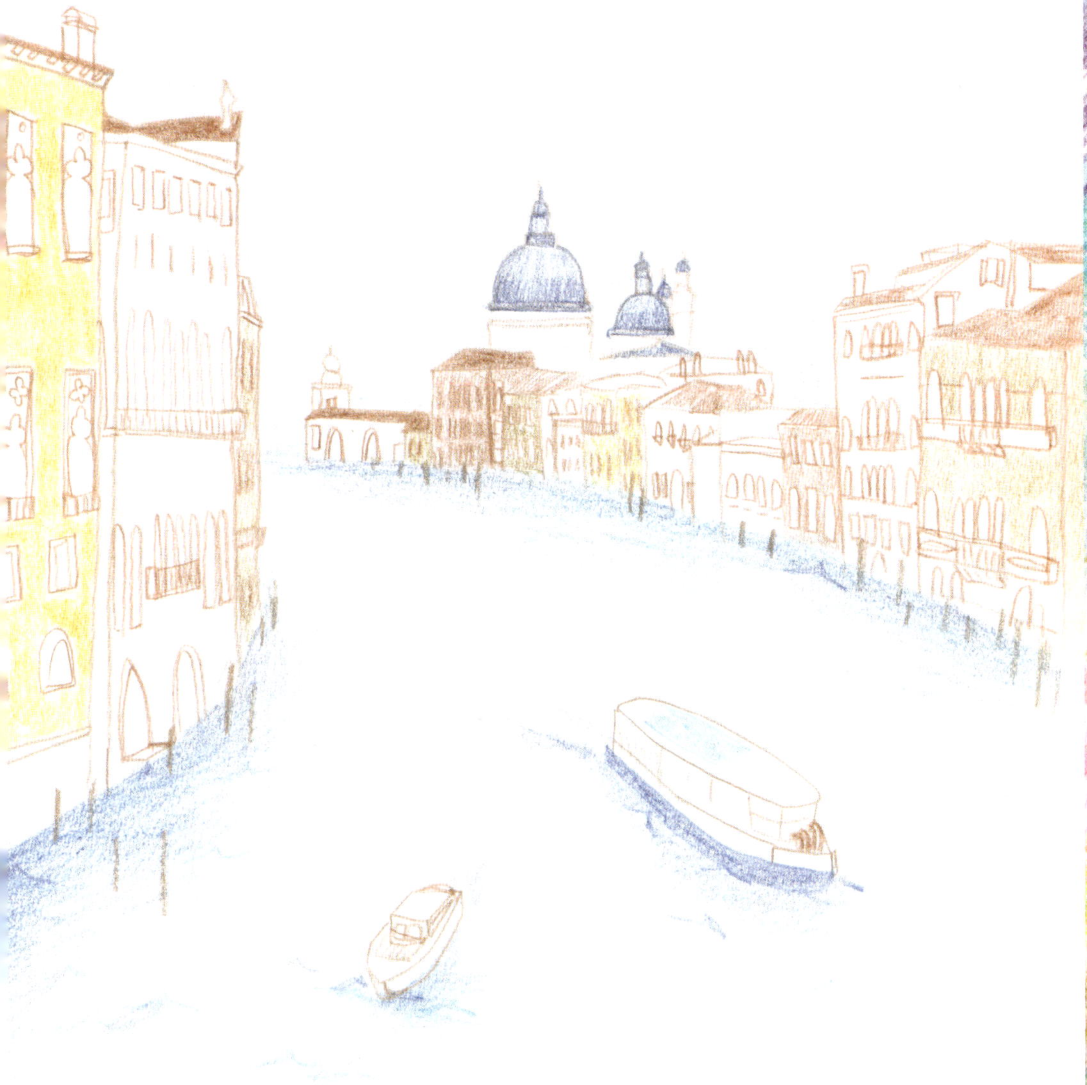

SKETCHING ON THE SPOT

Next time you go on an adventure, make sure to pack your sketching supplies. You never know when inspiration may strike, and it is highly likely to strike while you are doing something engaging in new surroundings!

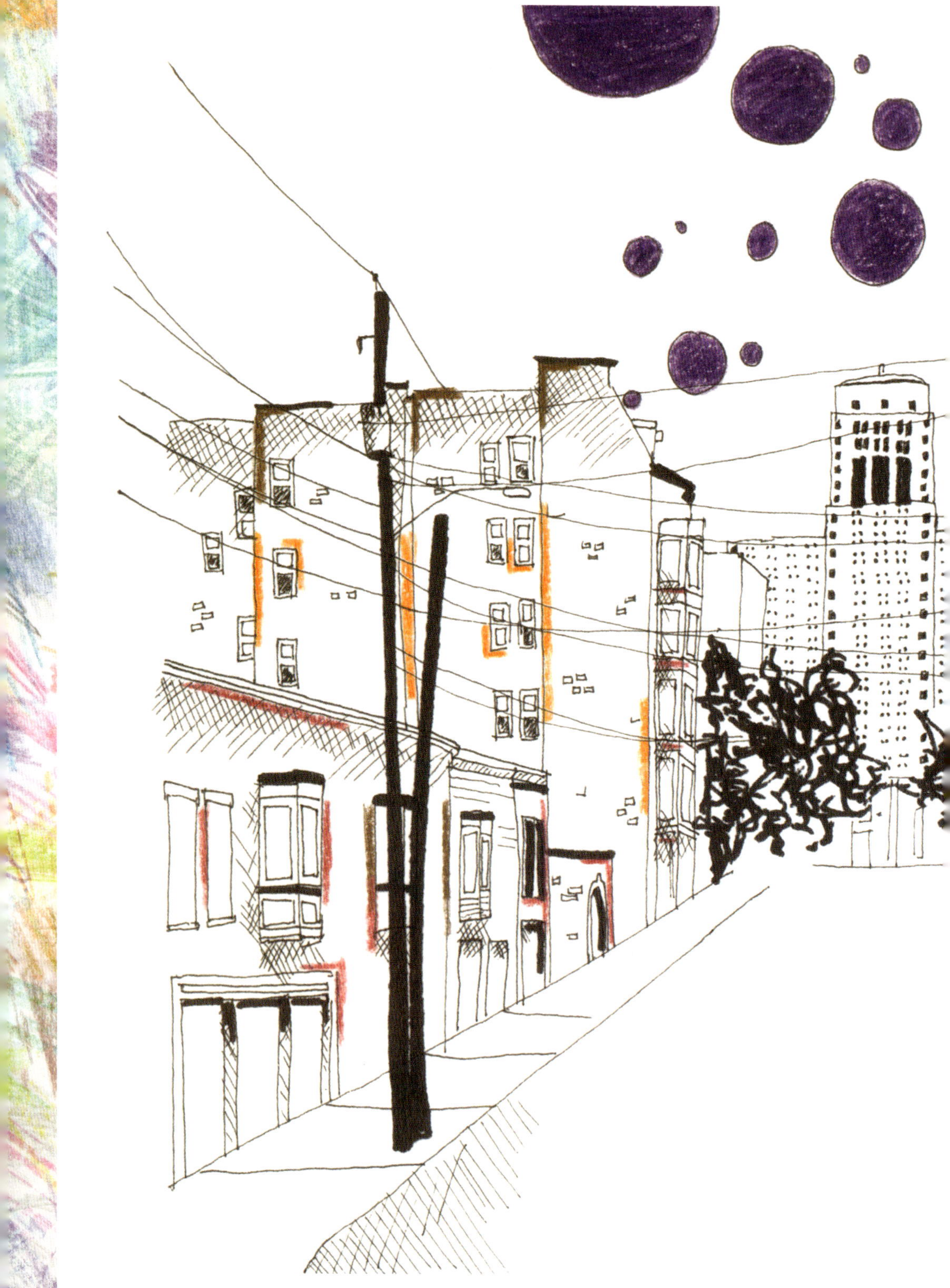

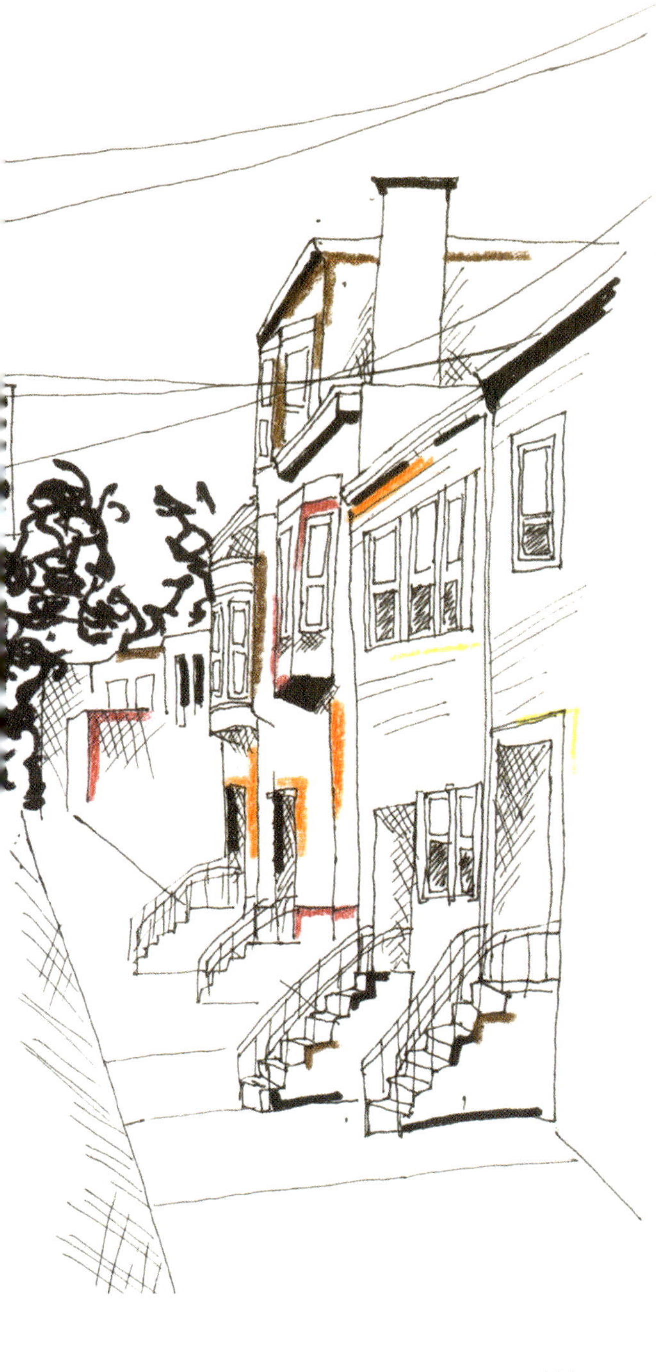

Colored pencil is a great medium for on-the-spot sketching. Once you've gotten the hang of drawing with colored pencil, why not add another medium? Pen and ink and watercolor are two mediums that are easy and popular to work with while out and about.

For more information on these and other mediums that you might want to combine with colored-pencil drawing, flip to the next page!

MIXING IT UP WITH MULTIMEDIA

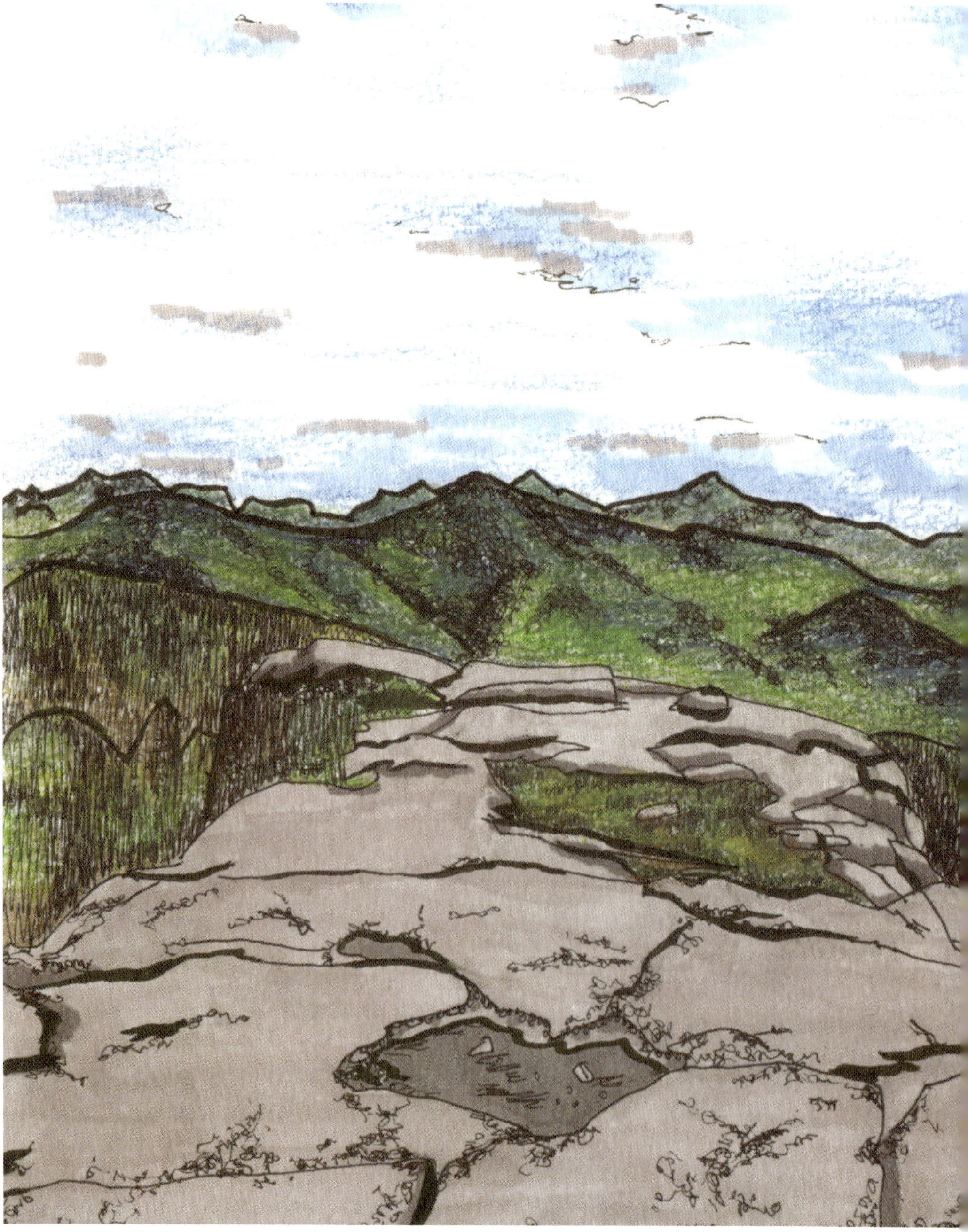

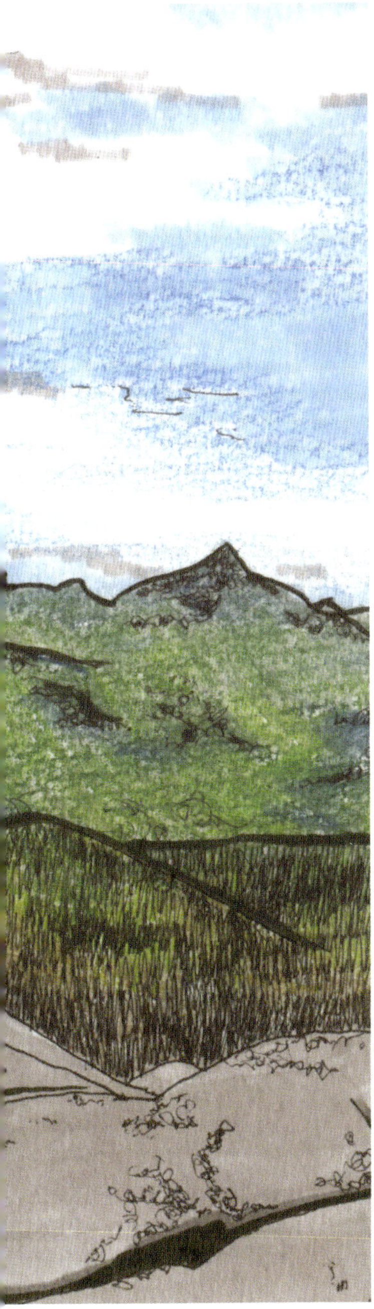

"Multimedia" means just that: multiple art mediums. Have you ever worked on an artwork and felt like you just couldn't get the effect you wanted with the one medium you were using? Fear no longer! Multimedia art allows you to stretch your horizons and use other mediums to create without limits.

When making multimedia art, you combine different art supplies to create an interesting and innovative effect. Some of my favorite mediums to combine with colored pencil are pen and ink, graphite pencil, and watercolor. However, you could use anything, from permanent markers and highlighters to an old white-out pen that adds an unexpected touch to your colored-pencil art. I've even seen people paint using their drip coffee!

Be creative; nothing is off limits!

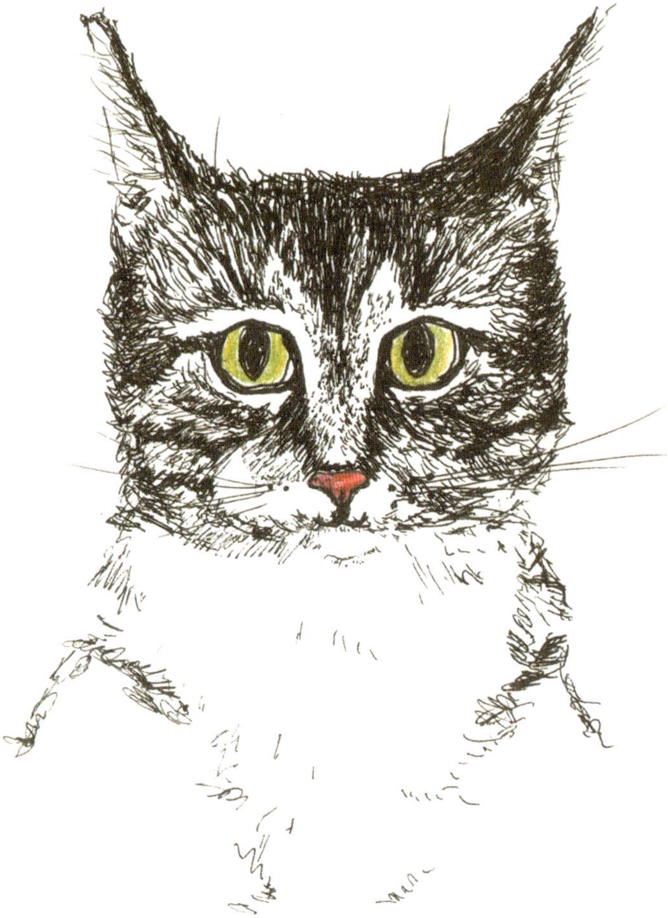

MEDIA MENTIONS

So, what types of mediums can you use with your colored pencils? Here are some ideas that I like to use:

I use **pen and ink** to bolden dark areas and create sharp contours in a drawing. Adding colored pencil to a pen-and-ink drawing contributes a fun pop of color!

The metallic, neutral quality of **graphite pencils** provides a subtle yet interesting complement to the more vibrant hues typically found in colored pencils.

Additionally, when a **watercolor** painting dries, you can add detail, sharpen edges, and deepen a color by going over the painted section with a colored pencil.

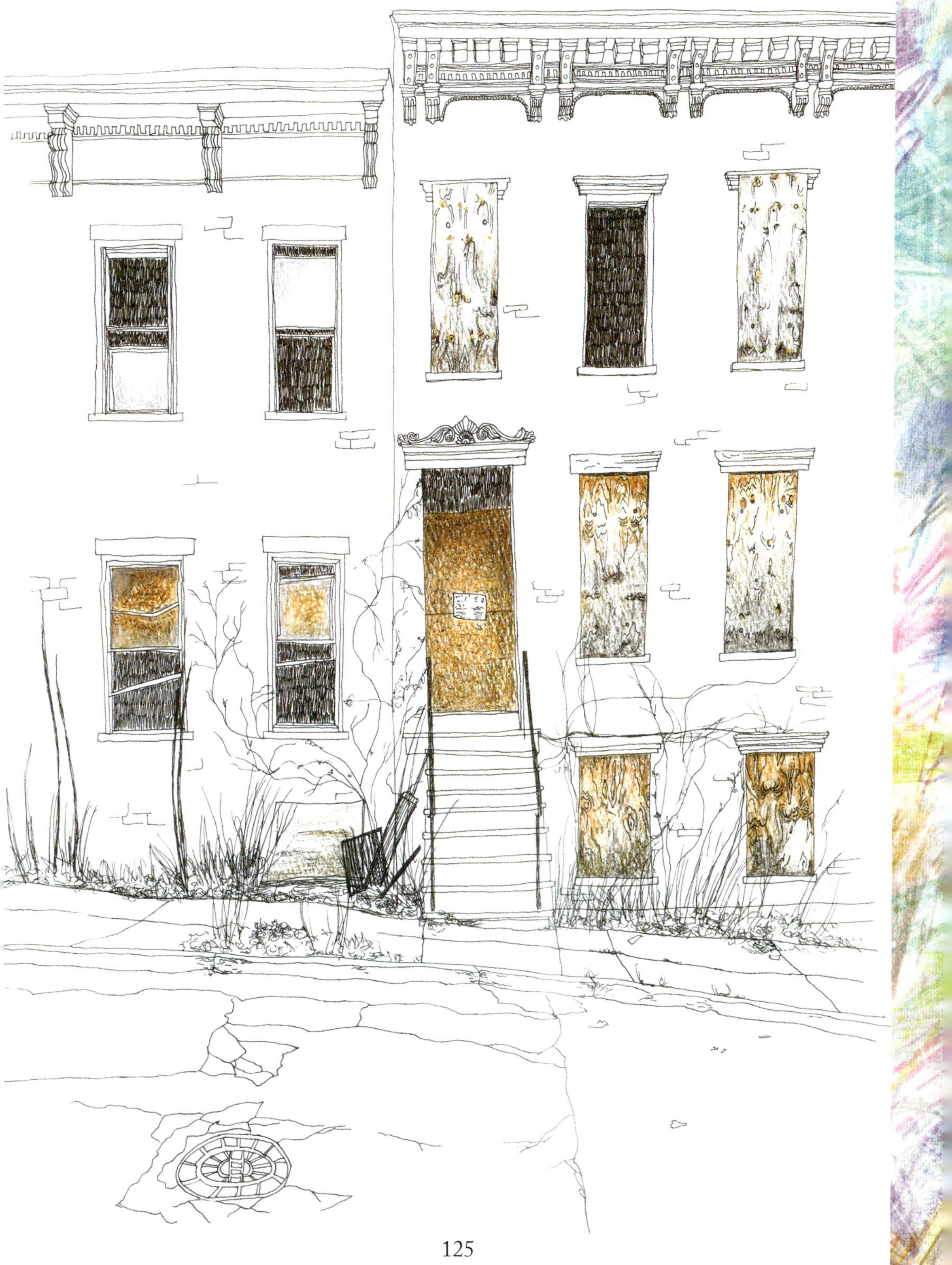

MORE ON MULTIMEDIA

It may be helpful to consider that you can create multimedia colored pencil art in two ways. The first way is to use colored pencil to add detail, saturation, and crispness to a base artwork that you have created using another medium, like watercolor.

The other way is to use different mediums for different areas of your artwork. You can see this here in my drawing of the potted succulent garden. Approximately half the plants and half the pots are done in watercolor; the rest are done in colored pencil. The two mediums do not overlap. This technique allows each medium to be showcased for its individuality and can create really interesting textures in your composition!

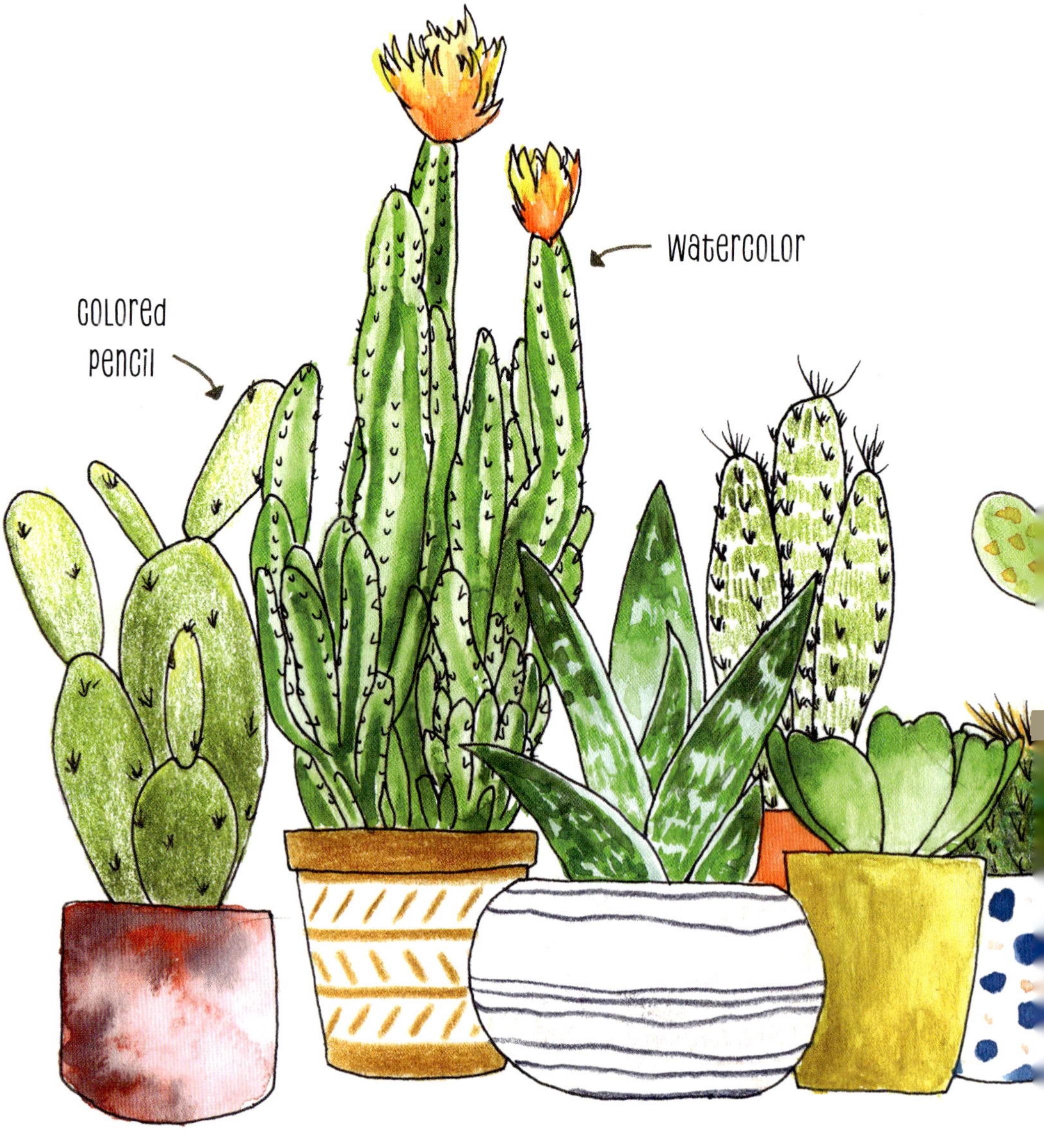

Perhaps the best part of making multimedia art is that you are not limited to using only one medium. Many artists even incorporate collage into multimedia pieces. Regardless of which additional mediums you choose, this is an excellent opportunity to expand your creative possibilities and experiment!

First I outlined each plant and pot with ink. Then I added color!

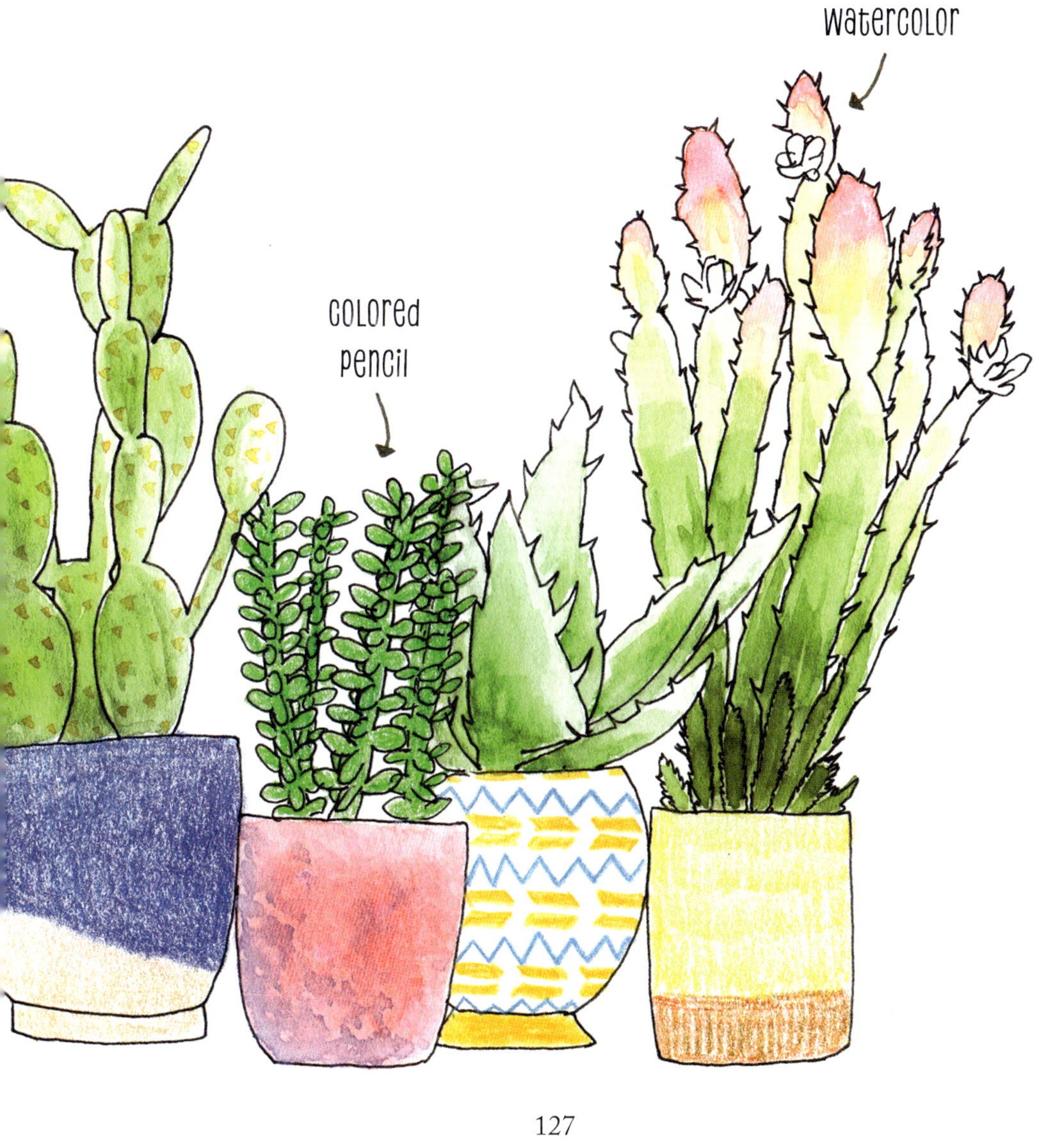

ABOUT THE AUTHOR

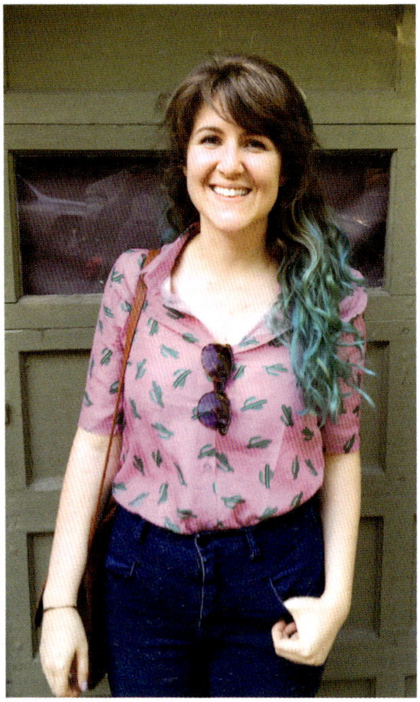

Cara Hanley is an illustrator living in upstate New York. Her training includes fine arts coursework at the School of Visual Arts in New York City and the University at Albany, as well as the artist residency program at the Scuola Internazionale di Grafica in Venice, Italy. Cara's extensive travels throughout Europe and North America have provided her with many valuable artistic influences.

Cara finds beauty and magic in the silence that exists between all of the "doing" in life. For Cara, this is life's essence, and it is what nourishes her soul. While she loves living and engaging in the energy of an urban environment, she also takes pleasure in moments of solitude—sipping a quiet cup of coffee in a busy café; reading books curled up on the couch with her cat, Zipper; or simply observing the stillness of urban architecture. Through her illustrations, Cara attempts to convey this sense of solitude and fulfillment and creates artwork that encourages introspection and mindfulness. Cara accomplishes this through the use of a variety of mediums, including colored pencil, pen and ink, watercolor, and gouache.

"I illustrate because it feels good to create."
–Cara Hanley